Moose in the Water
Bamboo on the Bench
A Journal and a Journey

by
Kathy Scott

With illustrations by
Michael Miling

Alder Creek Publishing

Printed in the United States of America

Illustrations by Michael Miling
Design by Jeanne Schultz

10 9 8 7 6 5 4 3

Library of Congress Cataloging-in-Publication Data

Scott, Kathy J., 1954–
    Moose in the Water Bamboo on the Bench
    A Journal and A Journey / Kathy Scott

    ISBN (Hard cover) 0-9657663-2-2

    1. Fly fishing. 2. Fishing rods–Design and construction.
    3. Nature writing. 4. Dogs–Anecdotes.

I. Title
799.1

00 135268
CIP

www.aldercreekpublishing.com

"For everything there is a season."

The Bible and The Byrds

Foreword

At first glance *Moose in the Water/Bamboo on the Bench* seems to be about making a split bamboo fly rod, but first impressions are often deceiving. Unlike a rod making manual, the charts, drawings, and taper tables are missing. Instead, the reader is offered prose, lyrics that tell a wonderful story-a story of how a rod maker, along with some trout and beaver, dogs, ducks, mice, and men, all help to craft a culm of Asian cane into a special fly rod-a rod that becomes a magic wand, a tapered shaft whose movement through the air has the power to take the angler to wilderness-a wilderness in which the cadence of casting mimics the motion of poplars and birch in an autumn breeze; mimics the repetitious roar of a waterfall and the rocking chair movement of a merganser's head as it swims across a quiet pond. Ah, Wildernesss! Ah, Nature!

But to make a split bamboo fly rod the craftsman must put aside nature. The craftsman must seek solitude and his craft indoors, step into a shop, stand at a bench, and leave the wild places behind. As one who has experienced wilderness, Kathy Scott understands that wilderness is not easily forgotten, not easily left behind. For with the search for solitude lies the other side of what this book is about, a solitude which is found in another wilderness, a second wilderness. In a special style, a graceful style, Scott informs us that there are two kinds of wilderness: wilderness of place and wilderness of time.

A high mountain lake, the depths of a cedar swamp, and the vast expanses of grassland or prairie are all wild places, all places where one can experience the solitude of wilderness. While on the other hand, temporal wilderness, wilderness of time, is found within our thoughts-found within our experiences-thoughts and experiences which make the solitude of the rod maker's bench truly a wilderness experience. For what more solitude is there than the lone craftsman toiling at a bench, working in silence just as a solitary river paddler pulls in harmony with the current of a Kennebec, Ausable, or Brule Brois. As the paddle swings, so does the plane iron. I have been to the wilderness, witnessed the fall of an eagle, heard the cry of a loon, and sat beside a mountain lake to commune only with God, all the while realizing that wilderness is contentment, wilderness is solitude, and wilderness can be lonely.

As a craftsman standing beside my bench, I have felt contentment, experienced a similar emotion to that which fills me while amid wild and natural surroundings. Serenity, solitude, and yes, exhilaration are enjoyed while standing at my bench holding a bamboo fly rod. A rod crafted by my own ability, with skills learned from old men. Men who asked only in return that I pass on the knowledge, pass on the magic. They understood; the old men understood the importance of wilderness, both of time and place.

Kathy Scott, in this wonderful story, shares with us not only the realization that wilderness can be a *Moose in the Water* but also, oh so much more so and perhaps equal to, *Bamboo on the Bench*! I applaud her insight and her humanity, for we all need wilderness and good people with whom to share! I invite you to enjoy this read; it is indeed a lovely read.

Ronald J. Barch

Preface

In the summer of 1998 my best friend, someone with whom I share everything, learned to make a split bamboo fly rod. Being also my husband and fishing partner, he gave his first bamboo fly rod to me. The rod was completed in the spring of 1999, and David soon began a second split cane rod. By the start of the second rod I realized I was hooked! I knew I had to learn about this mysterious and marvelous craft.

David began splitting the cane for the second rod on a glorious and "can't get any better than this" April morning. Immersion crafts, being what they are, he begged off from our daily hike together around the moose pond. Not one to miss out on a perfect spring day, the dogs and I hiked on our own. When I returned, David was as eager for the intimate details of our day as I was to hear of his. As we exchanged stories, I began jotting down his rodmaking comments. These notes were to become a record of a new phase in our lives together. My journal would record our rodmaking adventures, and we would grow to celebrate each detail while looking at them frozen on the written page.

Later, when David decided to give his second bamboo rod to a very good friend I was pleased and puzzled-puzzled as to what my contribution could be. "Why not give him your journal?" David asked, motioning to my notes. Four seasons later, with the rod and the journal complete, we gave both to our friend. Our yearlong adventure of learning and effort, time and friendship has grown to become this book, a journal which tells a story of both *Moose in the Water and Bamboo on the Bench*.

Kathy Scott

Acknowledgements

My thanks to David Van Burgel, for his unflagging support and advice; both were unlimited and excellent. Thanks, also, to Jenny Haney and Chris Hutchins for initial proofreading and unbridled enthusiasm, to Ron Barch from beginning to end, to Karla, Alan, and Lori for background support, and finally to our families, to our friends, and most of all, to those ever-patient makers of split bamboo fly rods.

Kathy Scott

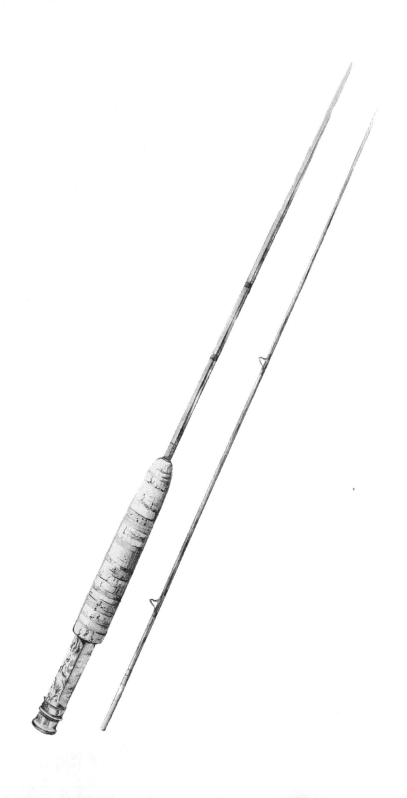

Part One

Spring

"When I was a kid I dreamed a thousand dreams of someday being on a river with a rod just like that."

Francis "Digger" DeGere
Portrait of a Rodmaker

April 19, Monday, 3:30 pm

The blackflies haven't arrived yet, but the breezes still feel good. During April in the Maine woods, 65 degrees and sunny is fairly warm. The pond looks more like a lake than the thirty acres of lilypads and beaver paths it becomes in summer. The dogs and I stopped at Bull Moose Cove on our walk two hours ago. There were no bull moose yet, but the pair of geese from the last few days was still around. I crouched by the water while the boys nosed along the shoreline, and the geese came over, mumbling as usual. They followed us back to the flooded forest we call the Valley of the Dead and came over to investigate when we'd reached the Big Rock Point. So far, the closest they'll approach is twenty-five feet.

David is splitting cane. Yesterday he flamed the six splits of the culm Ron Barch gave him over Christmas in Michigan, scorching the enamel side with a propane torch until it was a deep brown. Each split was an inch wide and had been labeled with a line or lines across the end of the underside to show where it fit in the spiral node arrangement of the eventual rod. Ron is as outgoing and friendly as he is thorough in his rodmaking. He is also the editor of *The Planing Form*, a newsletter devoted to split bamboo, and the maker who showed David his craft. To look at the two of them, they might be long lost brothers.

David hoped to build himself a rod with two tips, so, with luck, every split would need to be divided again into three. He sharpened a nail and drove it into an anchoring block through a node on the thinnest one, the determining piece in the three-split possibility, and pulled the cane apart with care. Probably too thin. At least he'll have spares from the others, which are splitting perfectly. It's a job which requires gloves, since pulling the cane through the driven nail is a splintery affair.

5:30 pm

I finished planting the northern high-bush blueberries in the upper part of the clearing. We have wild ones at the edge of the woods and throughout the property, but we thought these would give variety for the birds, and I just wanted to try them. They're not the large berry, domestic variety, and are supposed to taste wild. I don't think the birds will care, and I hope the snowshoe hares that enjoyed Grandma's tiny memorial tree don't like blueberries. I'm an optimist. When we planted tamaracks and pines, the moose pulled some of them up immediately, and snapped off more the first spring. The animals were here first, and remind us of that. Some of the natives seem to like the improvements we've made; snapping turtles use our driveway for caches of eighty eggs or more.

The tree swallows are back. They were claiming the west bluebird box this morning, and the chickadees and nuthatches have company at the feeders: juncos, white throated sparrows, and purple finches. The hooded mergansers have made a ruckus in the pond all day as they chase each other; the ring-necked ducks are much milder, and are often in groups. Wood ducks are usually down at the grass-covered dam now, but they fly off crying as soon as we approach the Valley of the Dead. The mallards seem almost domestic, comparatively, and I haven't seen black ducks today. I did see one great blue heron, but it didn't seem interested in the two old nests in the sentinel tree. There are occasional ravens passing by, and numerous crows, but I don't think they nest here like the mourning doves do.

Before David split the cane, he used a fishtail wood-worker's chisel on the inside of each piece to remove the diaphragm on the back of each node. Now, with all of it split, he's using a heat gun to scorch the nodes, and then a small vise to pinch them flat. The bamboo smells rich as he works. Shadows are long this evening, and the low light on the house shows off its cedar shingles against the blue sky and white clouds. For now, working outside on the picnic table is wonderful. Cirrus clouds came through earlier, bright artistic mares' tails. Bodes for a change in weather for tomorrow night.

It's amazing to look at the cane, Arundinaria amabilis, translated the lovely reed, and think it was growing like grass in China. The great difference between split bamboo and graphite rods is certainly that cane rods are made and graphite, as they say, are built. We watched craftsmen at Diamondback in Vermont roll the blanks for the artificial rods, but most builders assemble a graphite rod from the blank on. The cane rod maker must start from the plant, create the blank, then assemble the rod components.

David inspects each node on each of the sixteen strips before heating each one and putting it in the vise. He takes great care with the amount of pressure and length of time in the vise, then inspects each one again. If the heat has scorched off the lines which designate the order of the strips, I pause from watching the dogs and remark them. Kodiak keeps the nearby feeders free of squirrels while Duncan, our nephew lab, supervises. The pond is shimmering with golden diamonds. It's Monday of our April vacation.

April 20, Tuesday, 3:45 pm

Today is a contrast to yesterday–overcast, no breeze. The pond is like glass, and the ducks and beavers leave silver V's trailing behind them in the black water, or, in the case of the woodies, big concentric silver circles as they take flight crying. It's 65 degrees again, and still no bugs.

David needed time to work on the rod, so Kodiak, Duncan, and I walked alone at 2:30. I like to go as early as possible so that I don't disrupt the evening roost, but not so far off our usual after school time that I break the pattern for birds or dogs this vacation week.

The woodies left the Rock Point and the Valley of the Dead as we went by, but I stopped just before the Grass Dam and had a close view of two hooded mergansers. Then Kodiak crossed the dam and they fled. I was looking for turtles, having seen five painteds. They were sunning on a log across the pond on the west shore of the Valley of the Dead as we went down the east shore. I noticed a great blue heron looking nervous on a deadhead as I crossed the dam, in time for me to stop and freeze until he raised a leg to rest again, and I could continue. It takes about fifteen minutes to reach the Grass Dam and start north along the other shore. I spied on the turtles on the way by, six of various sizes. As we traveled, most of the ducks relocated farther north by the big dam.

Another fifteen minutes later, the dogs and I paused at the lean-to site, directly across from our clearing. With binoculars, I could see David working on the strips on the deck. We went on to Bull Moose Cove to check on the arbutus, which was still in bud. A beaver swam over to check us out, but we continued on into the cutover

5

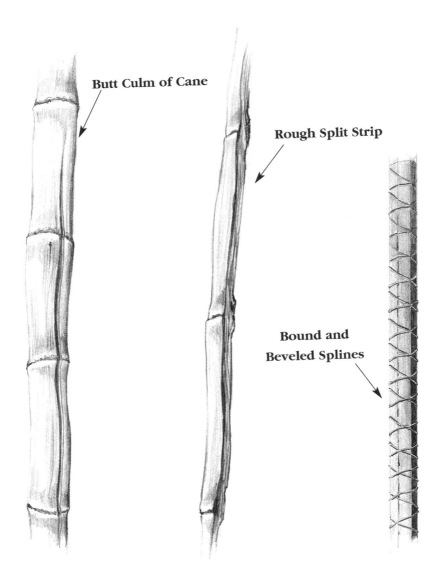

Butt Culm of Cane

Rough Split Strip

Bound and
Beveled Splines

behind our property, before worrying about sprinkles and turning back. The nuthatch which had been pecking a home-hole in Bull Moose Cove was gone when we returned. We've been watching it, high in a snag over the water close to shore, excavating the hole until it grows tired, or nervous, and stops to rest.

Back at the lean-to site, a silver wake appeared in front of us, and trailed behind the beaver the length of the pond, north to south, while a pair of geese flew by, reflected in the glassy water, south to north. I could see David look up, too, as they honked. Twice on the way back, I was close enough to wood ducks to see why they're called the jewels of the northern pond.

While we were gone, David took yesterday's strips out to the deck for an inspection and the next steps. There are no vise marks on them since he filed the teeth off the vise. He won't need all of the strips, hopefully, but spares can't hurt. Using a short section of a countertop, 3" by 18" formica and particle board with a square notch down its length, he planed the sixteen strips in the slot until each had a 90 degree edge. Then he switched to the wooden planing form he had made earlier to shape the 60 degree edges. Long slivers on an edge always need to be planed off because pulling them could cross over deep into the strip. He uses a Stanley professional plane with a Hock blade and wears leather gloves since the splinters, again, are brutal. Planed bamboo is very sharp. Each strip seems to rise out of the groove on the planing form as he moves along, and he's ever attentive to it. There's no part of this process which doesn't require concentration. The resulting strips are roughly 60 degree triangles, browned enamel on one side, that will need to be planed to the chosen taper.

He can continue now that the two dogs are lying down, greetings and inspections over. Both were pound puppies. Kodiak, who lives with us, has deep brown eyes in a cream colored face, a dark brown cape sprinkled with black, and ears that flop over backwards so that they change from dark to cream, and our friends are forever "fixing" them for him. He has the deep chest, endless endurance, and big paws of his sled dog ancestors, and a widow's peak like David. Duncan lives with David's sister a mile away but visits regularly for a swim in our pond. He's a chocolate lab. The two of them doze keeping one eye open to monitor the situation. There's a flicker nearby, this year's first, and the ducks are flapping down in the waters of the pond. It's still not raining at 4:30 pm.

This rod is David's second. The first he began last summer in Ron's class with two other aspiring rodmakers, and he finished it two weeks ago. He gave it to me before even splitting the culm, and I love it. We've only cast it in the yard, but it's amazingly responsive. I'm used to my 6-foot 3 weight graphite rod, my previous favorite, which I've used for everything from cutthroats to graying to brook trout to just messing around not catching a thing. I hope that the transition to this rod goes well.

Both cane rods are/will be Payne 97 tapers, seven feet long, 4/5 weight, unless David changes his mind on this one or earmarks it for our friend Coh. Although David gave me the 3 wt graphite rod for Christmas years ago, it was Coh who built it after the three of us spent a long evening hanging out in his rod shop. He hasn't actually said he'd like a cane rod, and David hasn't actually asked him, but there's an unspoken depth to their friendship that has lasted through time and across the miles that makes me believe Coh should start thinking about tapers pretty soon. In any event, it will be some version of a seven-foot rod, flamed brown.

Two ravens have come by; their rok carries a long way. One of them dropped what appeared to be a four-inch twig, and they both banked off and around and then disappeared into the evening.

Sometimes one side of the strip David is planing is too long, and he has to tilt the plane to get the 60-degree angle. He stops and shows me on the strip why he does it or shows me a particular node that is stubborn but may be resolved in the final planing. "You have to be careful when you're planing," he tells me. "This is the one thing that could ruin the entire rod." I can see that his eyes are twinkling.

April 22, Thursday noon, Earth Day

Yesterday David finished rough planing the 60 degrees into the strips. We paused to wait for an oven thermometer to arrive via UPS, and took off for the mountains. The weather here was partly cloudy, and it looked like a good day to do a little reconnaissance on a rumored short cut from the pond on the Caribou Valley paper company road, up past the spring on Spaulding Mountain, to our section of the Appalachian Trail. We volunteered to maintain a two mile length of ridgeline, clearing blowdowns and painting trail-markers, but access depends on driving back the logging road several miles, and then crossing a boulder strewn river and ascending a steep, two-hour pitch, before beginning work. Shaving some effort off the approach hike would sure help the maintenance energy when we topped out at the A.T.

Our plans didn't work out since a big chipper was left parked on the logging road only nine tenths of a mile in toward the pond. We were left to scout fishing holes on the Dead River and to discuss comments on the list serv from the various bamboo rodmakers. They're from all over the world, although usually only a handful take an active part. We're learning to distinguish rodmakers and weigh their advice. Ray Gould is always the sage, the voice of reason, and even his jokes about graphite are kind, if mischievous.

Today looks like a sunny, water-like-glass day, perfect for taking down the wood duck boxes that have sunk to water level. We were in the process of retrieving our canoe when Coh called from Michigan, where we grew up. The bamboo order is in, sounds like twelve foot culms. Ron and Coh will have to sort it out. We'll get ours this summer.

Talk has switched to the State's black bear and lynx research; we listened to a state biologist speak at the Western Maine Audubon meeting last night. The lynx research was the most revealing. The state needed to know if Maine lynx are residents, and therefore potentials for the Endangered Species Act, or Canadian residents and, therefore, not a concern here. To find out, they attempted to radio collar lynx last winter, choosing sites just four miles in from the Quebec border. They did finally collar a lynx, (There must be at least two since it now has young) but it hasn't managed to wander across the border yet.

April 23, Friday, 11 am

We took most of the day off from rodmaking to continue work on the wood duck box situation. When we put the boxes up three winters ago, we were concerned that the metal posts could tip in the soft floor of the pond, so we dropped a cement block over each shaft before bolting the box to the top. Whether that did it, or just from the weight of the boxes, three have sunken straight down to the point that the backboard touches the water, and one has wet nesting material inside. Yesterday, we canoed out to check their status and brought the most water-logged in to dry. Today, we finished making the extensions, but it's too windy to canoe back out. David did set the preliminary adjustments on the planing form.

April 24, Saturday, 8 pm

The test on the Neunemann oven David built for drying the bamboo strips was a success. (See *The Best of the Planing Form*, Barch/McKeon, pages 80-82.) I held the thermometer while David directed the heat gun, and it maintained 350 degrees for ten minutes with little trouble.

We're getting about twenty-five messages a day from the rodmakers' list serv, which is great fun.

Since it was very windy again this morning, but sunny, we went tote road hiking between East and Pierce Ponds. This is the route followed by the ill-fated Revolutionary War march on Quebec led by Benedict Arnold. Many Mainers have an appreciation for his efforts in these woods that seems to completely overshadow his later notoriety. We didn't see the usual bear tracks, but we did find a way to interconnect the logging roads between Bingham and North New Portland.

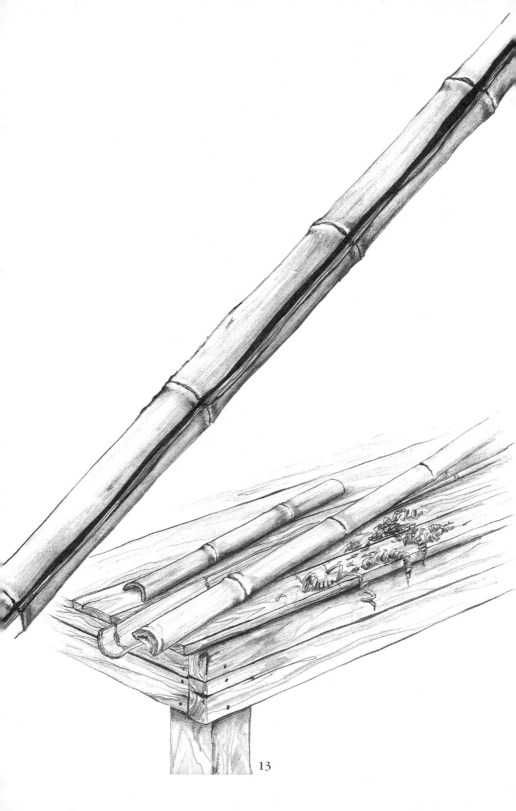

13

April 25, Sunday, 4 pm

It's a bit less windy, and still sunny, so we canoed out to extend the duck boxes. There was enough of a steady breeze to make it logistically and domestically challenging to attach the post extensions and re-attach the heavy boxes until we found our sea legs and worked out our method. We finished the box just out from the foot of our hill and then canoed (and were blown) across to Duck Cove. We used half of a discarded street signpost to extend that one. The water is very clear; the lilypads are just forming below the surface.

We canoed north to extend the boxes near either end of the big dam but opened one only to have a wood duck explode out. Her eggs looked warm and cozy, and we beat a hasty retreat to the opposite box, only to flush out a second wood duck. As we withdrew, several ring-necks and a pair of hooded mergansers flew over the dam, chased by a large falcon. It could be a brown phase gyrfalcon; a white one came through two years ago at this time.

Although the oven is ready, David is using the metal planing form to reduce strip sides to .2" before heat treating them. It gives him a chance to look them over again, and he has selected the six butt strips and the six tip strips he wants, banding them together with labeled masking tape.

Coh called last night to talk about the twelve-foot culms of cane. He now has it in hand, having retrieved it over a few beers with Ron the evening before. Although we want ours left in twelve foot lengths, Coh is going to cut his in half for shipping. Some of his graphite clients want a single culm; bamboo is a curiosity.

April 27, Tuesday, 8:30 pm

It's chilly but sunny again after yesterday's brief showers and light hail. I walked with Kodiak while David planed the tips to get them ever nearer (0.150") to the finished size before using the oven. After planing a set, he lays them in order, marked by felt marker again with one to six little parallel lines. He lays them across a piece of masking tape, then curls them into a hexagon and binds them with cotton thread. He twists the thread to the tip in half-inch increments, and then spirals it back down. He leaves a thread loop extended from either end so that the rod tip or butt can be lowered into the oven and hung afterward.

The first painted trillium was out by the rock wall west of Bull Moose Cove today. The trailing arbutus near the cove is out, too. It's a bit windy for the ducks, but five ring-necks are still fretting over our presence in their territory. Kodiak and I went behind our property to the Hampshire Hill tote road, then hiked up past the granite foundation that marks the old Kimball's mill site to check the two spring holes. I found the springs dry! Usually their water holds hundreds of frogs' eggs which now have become casualties of the uncommonly dry weather. Maybe the black flies will be too.

April 28, Wednesday, 8:30 pm

David continued hand planing the bevel on the tip strips while I walked the dogs. The breeze is still keeping the blackflies down. A hooded merganser came out of the box nearest the Big Rock, joined its mate, and flew off complaining when we went by. We paused at Bull Moose Cove to look over the glorious patch of trailing arbutus; a moose had kicked free some blossoms, so I picked up one tiny bunch for David. The nuthatch is still working; its hole is so deep that only the tip of its tailfeathers shows when it's inside.

The beavers are shoring up the Grass Dam, where the trail crosses on the southern end of the pond. On our way back from the cove, we bushwacked upstream to see if they're at risk of flooding a neighbor's land. We close our land to trapping; although we make no attempt to tame them, we've habituated our beavers to human presence, so we owe them at least that much. Besides, we enjoy watching them. There are neighbors who would like their pelts, so maintaining a low flooding profile is in the beavers' best interest if we're going to keep the peace. There are long mazes of dams intertwined with the alders and continuing far upstream, but they're all still on our land.

May 2, Sunday, 5 pm

David finished the adaptations to the bamboo oven, a copper extension which holds the heat gun securely and a deflector so that the exiting heat doesn't hit the gun. He's been working on it, or the strips, off and on since Wednesday. Meanwhile, the weather continues to be sunny and dry, the driest April on record. The spring peepers are in grand chorus, though, and leaves are coming out. White-throated sparrows, goldfinches, and robins were singing all day, and the tree swallows were harvesting the pesky blackflies. Blackflies always show up eventually.

Kodiak and I went wading south of the Grass Dam toward the beaver mazes on Friday afternoon, trying to see a bittern pumping. We hadn't actually meant to wade, but it did beat crawling through alders in the heat and dealing with biting blackflies, and the water was only knee deep.

Heat treating the cane bundles today seems to have been successful. David adjusted the heat gun to sustain 350 degrees throughout the length of the oven, using the probe in test holes in the middle and at the bottom to monitor the temperature. He suspended the tip and butt bundles into the oven from a heavy gauge crosswire. After ten minutes, he reversed the bundles to make up for any temperature variation, and treated them for another ten minutes. "Getting this right is important," he teases when I seem far too serious with the clock. "This could be the one thing that ruins the entire rod, you know!"

While he hanged the bundles on the clothesline to cool a bit, he put the open rod case out in the sun. It was a good drying day. When the bundles reached the ambient temperature, he put them in the rod case and screwed on the cap.

May 3, Monday, 7 pm

There are enough blackflies now to make it miserable standing still, but the slightest breeze, even from walking, keeps them at bay. The wild oats were out on our way to the Grass Dam. The beavers are still shoring that dam up, even with this drought. Maybe rains had kept their work curtailed during wetter years, flushing some of it through.

We turned back from our walk at the lean-to site. We may put a lean-to there someday, overlooking the pond, but, more likely, it just has the potential to be a great site for a lean-to. Perched among the firs and hemlocks, the clearing is ideal for scouting for wildlife. There was a cow moose ahead in Bull Moose Cove. The vegetation is just starting to grow under water, and the blackflies must plague her, so we didn't want to intrude. At least, I didn't want to; Kodiak and Duncan may have wanted to, given good opportunity.

On the way back, I tried to show the dogs a frog at the Big Rock. We all stood in the water, and I pointed it out. Both dogs wanted to find it, but couldn't see it or smell it, apparently, at three inches from their eager noses. It must not be in their scent repertoire. When he rides in our car, Kodiak works his sixty pounds up on to my lap, closer to the air vent. He's keenly absorbed with the scents in that nose radio, and always looks up to spot the dog moments after we've sped past it.

David fired up the router, and put a sixty-degree bevel on the edges of some one-inch wide cedar strips he had planed. He laid the six strips across masking tape, much like a rod blank in progress, and spread wood glue down the beveled edges. Then he rolled them into a hexagon and wrapped a spiral of string up their length for drying.

The intent is to make a rod case of cedar. Afterward, he washed off the excess glue, and let it dry on the picnic table for an hour while we retreated indoors. At the end of the hour, he took off the string, only to find that it had cut into the edges at every wrap. It's disappointing; it must be that cedar is too soft.

Now, he's outside, trying to sand the remaining glue off and experimenting to see if the string marks can be sanded off, too. He has maple strips to try and is considering big flat rubber bands instead of string. Kodes and I can hear the white throats around him through the window where we're watching his progress. I go out and help when I can, but stay out of the bugs otherwise.

David was pleased with the Vo Tech School's job of shaping a ten-inch hexagonal steel rod into a 1/4" to 7/8" taper. He tried out the new tool by putting a round winding check on it and using a vise to pinch the winding check into a hex shape. My rod has a circular check.

Today we picked up a maple board for mounting our small lathe for storage in a plastic transport box. It may travel a bit this summer, but David won't be taking it to the Northeastern Bamboo Builders' Gathering, (better known as The Grand Gathering), in three weeks since we've decided that he'll fly. He's been corresponding with Ted Knott, who seems to be coordinating the event. It sounds like it would be a shame to drive out alone and be too tired to take in all the information. I won't get back from an extended field trip to Prince Edward Island until after we'd have to leave to drive, and the gathering is on the Grand River, out past Toronto. Maybe next time we'll drive there together.

The breeze and occasional sprinkles kept the blackflies down to tolerable for our walk today. I was excited to find showy lady's slippers before their flowers actually open; I'd been wondering what they look like when they first come up. The cow moose was back in Bull Moose Cove. I watched her from the lean-to site with binoculars, trying to see any visible hint of a nursing calf. Her shoulders are shiny and slick where the winter hair has finally rubbed off. Despite her obliging poses, the jury is out on the existence of a calf.

May 23, Sunday, 4pm

Rodmaking has had to take a backseat to related, and unrelated, pursuits. We've been reading the list serv every day, but we had to have a boatbuilder check the wooden Old Town runabout we inherited for repairs. My five day PEI trip starts tomorrow, and David's rodmakers' gathering follows it over Memorial Day weekend. Plans are brewing for a friend to come out from Michigan then. In other words, there's been no progress on the rod.

Meanwhile, we've also mowed our so-called lawn twice, and the lilypads are back with all kinds of frogs to keep them company and add a new chorus to the night. The mountain ash is blossoming, and the Hawthorne's blossoms will burst open any time. The phoebes have eggs in a nest on the porch roof support over our front door. A hummingbird thoroughly inspected my red striped shirt this morning, and today's breezes are keeping the blackflies down. I'm amazed at how many lady's slippers we've found. I'm still watering the highbush blueberries we planted, but rain is threatening.

David and I will be apart for eight days, the longest we've been apart in twenty-four years. I wish it was possible for both of us to go both places.

June 12, Saturday, 6pm

Rodwork has been peripheral for some time as spring turns into summer. I went off to Nova Scotia and Prince Edward Island with my students for a week, and David left for Ontario just before I returned. Our friend Janet left husband Coh and their girls at home and came out from Michigan to tromp our paths. Coh, David, and I had once pooled our meager resources and financed one of those college student-backpacking jaunts to the British Isles. We had flown back as far as Canada when the money ran out, so we split up at the Michigan border. We were to rendezvous at the apartment David's sister Barb shared with her roommate, Janet. Coh arrived there first, and the rest is history. Barb lives about a mile north of us now, with Duncan, and teamed up with Janet and me to rehash their days as roommates and share assorted local stomping grounds until David returned.

David and I won the bid on a larger lathe at the Vo Tech school and spent this afternoon unloading it for storage in Barb's barn. She indulges our toys. Eventually, we hope to make all of a rod's components. It's our third lathe. I wonder if you need the same number of lathes as you do canoes: one more.

David caught five browns and a bass in Canada with my rod, it's initial experience. He was reluctant to be the first to use it, but I was happy with the arrangement. He made the rod.

The phoebe chicks over the front door are so big that they're overflowing the nest. The pond is choked with lilypads, and the turtles have lain eggs in the yard. The lady's slippers are gone, but the irises are out. So are the bunchberry blossoms, white stars above green leaves carpeting the path by the Grass Dam. There are green blueberries on the bushes. We've mowed the clearing four times, and last week had record breaking heat.

David ordered insulation for the bamboo oven, and re-copied the Medved beveler plans. He's curious about its ability to shave time off planing strips; he saw it demonstrated at the Grand Gathering. Building one would be easier in a well-equipped shop; maybe he can make one with his brother. We go to Michigan soon.

June 20, Sunday, 2 am

It's the last day of spring, or will be at sun-up. Monday will be the first day of our summer vacation if we finish packing today. Rodmaking has been somewhat over-shadowed by the end of the school year, packing for Michigan, and musing over the freedom of the second half of the summer. How should we spend it? Back to the Rockies? Labrador and Newfoundland? Northern Ontario? I'd like to be conservative since David's back is still healing from a February injury, but there's a lot to do without wrestling canoes or heavy backpacks this summer.

The ideas on the rodmakers' list serv, and those still surfacing from the Grand Gathering, fill idle thoughts with evolving techniques. David still isn't satisfied with the oven's performance, so he ordered some 1" thick, five-inch diameter pipe insulation. He made an interesting friend of the clerk in the plumbing shop, but the insulation was a setback. It only comes in six-inch diameters. Now he'll have to re-build the exterior of the oven, probably in Michigan.

We have decided to wrap the twelve-foot culms of bamboo with a tarp in August and transport it on the roof rack back to Maine, rather than pull the trailer to Michigan.

I had three days here after my school ended while David still worked. Although I cleaned, packed gear, and ran errands, it was still a wonderful luxury to enjoy the last days of spring. The greens are lush and vibrant now, and the birds make the trees seem more alive. Kodiak and I sat at the picnic table watching rose-breasted grosbeaks mine the ground beneath the feeders for lost seeds, birds as tame as they are striking. Chickadees shared the feeders with nuthatches, annoyed with the reluctance of their fledglings to fly to the seeds and feed themselves, and with purple finches, always selfish with the perches. In the firs, catbirds alternated between their feline calls and the melodious songs that give a clue to their relationship with mockingbirds. The robins fledged young in the center stand of firs. The little phoebes, still overflowing their nest, are courageous when the screen door slams. I think they'll be off in the next day or so, and it'll be safe to step out on to the deck below them in bare feet again.

Wednesday, I walked Duncan and Kodiak around the pond to the lean-to site. There were sixteen large grayish feathers on the Grass Dam. I wonder if a heron has met its end or if a goose has molted. At the shore below the lean-to site I could see a great blue heron standing on a log out by the beaver house. Unfortunately, it was in the landing pattern for a swallow's nest in a flooded tree. The heron was remarkably agile at ducking.

I was quite absorbed when Duncan stepped through some ferns into a beaver access channel and became immediately mired. He was quite calm about it. He just sat dolefully waiting for me to wade out behind him and lift up those poor old, deteriorating hips of his. That idea seemed like a last option to me. I leaned out and snagged his collar, but the suggestion of me pulling him out that way just made him sigh and roll his eyes. Labs! Since we weigh about the same, it was a bit unrealistic. Still tethered to his collar, I finally worked my way to the opposite point of the channel, which turned him on to his stronger leg, and "we" extracted him from the muck.

I decided to put off watching herons and searching for bullfrogs and took to the ridge, with Duncan none the worse for wear. Kodiak had disappeared, but when I called came running with the gift of a limp baby snow-shoe hare, which he plopped at my feet. It's hard to scold a dog bearing gifts. The hare was at that cutest stage in bunny life, just mobile and still a baby. I laid it safely to rest in the blackberry brambles near-by, where Kodiak wouldn't re-think the loss.

Kodiak is bright, but easily duped. We were walking that same ridge back toward the Grass Dam today when he suddenly pounced into the forest duff at the base of some stump-sprout maples. It was chaos. Everything was flying in the air: ferns, leaves, dirt, a panic-stricken chipmunk. The commotion was all the more raucous between Kodiak's frustration and the chipmunk's fright. If it hadn't been a life or death battle, I would have laughed out loud.

And then it stopped. Kodiak froze, staring at the ground. I looked, too. Then I noticed, inches above his head, an adolescent chipmunk on the thin trunk, making a reach for a branch. It missed. My heart sank, but then it hooked one elbow over the tiny branch.

So there they were, Kodiak intent on the empty ground and the chipmunk within his reach, swaying back and forth by an elbow just above his head. It was hard to breathe, and, not knowing the outcome, hard to decide whether to laugh, intervene, or freeze. I froze. The chipmunk used all its strength, little shoulder muscles straining, and grasped the tiny limb with its other paw. It gained the limb, followed the twigs to the next maple, and was gone. Kodiak gave the ground a few pokes with his paw and gave up.

I almost hate to leave this place to go to Michigan, but I can't wait to go there. Our family farm in Northern Michigan is one thousand acres of past memories and present joys. Our siblings (except Barb), parents, friends, and neighbors are still there, and so are the big pine my older brother and I climbed to the top as children, the fields my grandfather cleared, the house where Grandma made cookies, and the wooded cemeteries where those three lie. David's mom makes the cookies now, and I can't wait to feel her hugs. My mother and step-father will make a point to come up from Florida, so we'll all be home. Michigan is a different place outdoors from Maine, special in different ways. I love the woods, the cattle and horses, the hayfields, the deer and turkeys. Of course, David and I are also excited by the endless possibilities for adventures the second half of the summer holds. We may even get in a little rodmaking.

Part Two

Summer

July 3, Saturday, 11 pm

We spent the first night in Michigan with Janet and Coh. Friends usually share a lot of good memories, but good friends usually share some disasters. Janet spent an agonizing night in an emergency room once and later told me that she'd only had three worse experiences. They were all with us.

We've been lost together twice, although the first time we were with three other people. Janet and Coh had come out from Michigan with another good friend, Crewf. Barb, David, and I were recent transplants and lived on the northern border of Maine in a small French town at the edge of the seemingly endless woods. A local guy had offered to show us a hidden trout lake, so we seven went to scout it before breakfast at the nearby diner. As it happened, he had a much better idea of the route down the wooded bowl to the lake than of the route back. We had abdicated all responsibility, so we couldn't complain as the hours passed and darkness fell. About then, one of those cold, October drizzles moved in. We had one book of matches among us, but managed to get a fire going.

It was a pretty cheerless fire. No one's jokes were funny. The timing was terrible for all females involved. The three smokers had left their cigarettes in the car and weren't amused when we pointed out the golden opportunity to quit. David and I might have been the best prepared, mentally, since we'd just finished a month straight on the Appalachian Trail, but we were a bit mortified at the fate we'd bestowed on our visiting friends. Besides, Janet and Coh had the only food, a fireball, which they kept for themselves and shared the hard way. Our local friend turned hero the next morning by hot-footing toward the noise of a chainsaw, and keeping it revving until we'd all found the road.

I'd like to think we all learned something from that experience. A summer or two later, the four of us were lost again, although I prefer to believe that we were just disoriented and used our sharp wits to save ourselves. We were in a maze of lakes in Minnesota's Boundary Waters and mistook an island for a peninsula. We finally just quit paddling and rafted up, mid-lake. We had maps and compasses, but nothing looked right. Maybe we would have figured it out, but another canoe appeared in the distance. Janet was on her feet, waving, and we piped in. The president of a midwest university and his companion patiently pointed out our location on our map. We were within sight of our last campsite.

Hoping to foolproof a subsequent trip, David and I drove to Wyoming a couple of weeks before Janet and Coh were free. We found a convenient motel and reserved a cabin in advance, then called our hiking partners to arrange the rendezvous. We'd been back-packing in the Wind Rivers before but planned to test run all possible trails and campsites before they arrived.

Two days later, we set up a tent at the first potential site, an alpine lake with good shelter back in the trees and a nearby stream for water. Just before dusk, the glassy surface dimpled with rising trout. We thought we'd better try the fishing so we could report back to Coh, and found a couple of good locations on the shore. I took the one nearer the rocks, and I worked my way out through some small tundra willows until I could step up on a boulder and scout the situation. David had caught and released two small trout before I had negotiated a cast, and it looked like it would be dark if I didn't hurry. I just got some line out and had identified my target when I snagged the fly in the backcast. I wasn't happy.

As the clock ticked away, I traced the line back into the willows. It went around and around the low branches and then down a hole. I thought it seemed odd and was lying on my stomach with my arm down the hole when David quit for the night and came over. My fingers slid down the line to its fuzzy end, and I extract-ed my fly, mouse attached. I had the poor thing by just the ruff of the neck, and he seemed pooped; he was probably reconsidering willow as a supper dish. He hanged there like a kitten while I removed the fly and let him go. We looked for better water the next day; Coh might not be satisfied with catch and release mouse fishing.

On the pre-arranged day, we headed to the cabin for an early shower and a nap before our friends arrived. We just made it since the proprietor told us the town would be shutting off the water until evening for servicing. Janet and Coh were right on time that night. We all went out to a big supper and an equally big breakfast before retrieving our packs from the motel, filling our water bottles, and starting our climb. We perched our tents together two hundred feet from the shore of a promising lake.

About midnight, something went terribly wrong. I barely unzipped our tent before I was sick and convulsing. David sat up and rubbed my back, and I tried to imagine what Janet and Coh must be thinking next door. It somehow struck me as funny, although I doubt if my laughter improved the situation. After I collapsed back into my sleeping bag the second time, compassionate voices from the next tent offered to do whatever they could, but there was nothing to be done.

Before I unzipped the tent for the third time, Coh was rocketing out of his. As the night went on, he was draped over a log having conversations with a guy in an eagle-feather headdress, and Janet and David could see the handwriting on the wall. The sky clouded over by dawn, and David was the next to go. He just lay in the tent, miserable, and I had recovered enough to be a perfect match. Coh was inside his tent, too, and Janet was mixing sugared drinks with a pinch of salt in an effort to re-hydrate us. Pattering had started on the tent when she handed us our water bottle. We thought it might be raining. She sighed when she told us. It was snow and hail.

Coh was up fishing in the morning, pale but undaunted, and David and I were ready to continue the trip. We accepted the reasoning of the last potential victim, though. After the best fish breakfast we'd ever eaten, we headed down. The story couldn't just end there. As we were driving from the trailhead to the highway, a dog jumped out in front of their car. They swerved and missed it but weren't so lucky with a small boulder hidden behind the sagebrush. Of course, no one in town could fix the wheel. Janet just made it to the motel.

Fortunately, we have more good times than hard luck stories. Catching up took us into the late hours so it wasn't until midnight that we could head down to the shop to check things out. Coh has the ideal job; he whole-sales rod building supplies out of an old friend-friendly warehouse near his home. It was pretty late when eventually we all dozed while watching the now classic film *A River Runs Through It* on cable TV, a novelty for us. It had been a long day and as Paul was "shadow casting" I couldn't keep my eyes open.

In the morning, we looked over the twelve-foot culms at the shop and cast cane rods until we thought we should head the last hundred miles north and Coh should get a little work done.

Unpacking took a back seat to a quick round of visiting the families, and we were off to Grayrock early Friday morning. Grayrock, organized by Wayne Cattanach and other dedicated rodmakers is the laid back, Michigan rodmakers' gathering, similar to the Grand Gathering David took in over Memorial Day weekend. The Rodmakers converge on Grayling with the Trout Bums and Fish Heads during the hexagenia hatch exchanging rodmaking ideas, fishing, and according to the mythology, consuming single malt scotch. Two of those three are definitely true. On the final night, the Trout Bums' Barbecue raises funds earmarked for stream restoration projects by Trout Unlimited; the rodmakers contribute by offering a cane rod for auction with component sections made by twenty-eight different craftsmen.

T.U. was born there in Grayling, on the shores of the Au Sable River.

I had once been assured that women need not be intimidated at a gathering and that it was a great place to cast rods. Even so I still approached it apprehensively, and I didn't want my presence to detract from the experience for David. It was a makers' gathering, after all, and I hadn't made a rod. We were very early arrivals, "Eastern Grayrock Time," and rodmakers who'd been fishing all night drifted in about ten. Everyone was friendly, and we spent the better part of two days there.

Nothing was rushed, but there was so much to learn. Importers Harold and Eileen Demarest talked of cane and China, shared pictures, history, and lore. Al Medved demonstrated his beveler while we visited with Carole and their bulldog, Clara. Later on another rodmaker demonstrated flaming a culm to a Paul Young brown. A wholesaler offered forty percent off components if ordered over the next two weeks, so we spent this morning at the farm concocting our order: reel seats, ferrules, hex shaped winding checks. I was only a little shy casting a new rod over the Au Sable, between the aluminum hatches and the other very kind rodmakers looking on. One of them handed me an original Leonard to cast. A Maine legend, Hiram Leonard, inspired awe in Henry David Thoreau for his outdoor prowess. Like Charles Wheeler from Farmington, Bangor's Leonard was honored for his six-strip bamboo rods in the 1870's. His apprentices included Fred E. Thomas and Edward Payne, whose legacies are well-known in the cane world.

The highlight of my first gathering, though, was overhearing Medved tell Mike Biondo, the list serv maintainer, how he'd seen David's first rod at the

Grand Gathering and that it was as if he'd already made one hundred. Biondo was equally gracious when he examined it later, as others had been the day before. With so much heart in that rod, a little praise felt good. I'm convinced that these rodmakers are the nicest, least selfish, most encouraging people I've met. Split cane rodmakers seem to come from every walk of life, but I've found the second thing they have in common. Whether the pilot letting us cast his vintage Leonard or the guidance councelor sharing techniques, they were wonderful.

July 12, Monday, 7 pm

Eventually, a rodmaker has to choose between the many tapers available and set the planing form. David had been debating but had gone as far with this rod as he could before facing the moment of truth. The new rod will be Coh's, who was pleasantly amazed when he cast my Payne 97 on Thursday. David and Coh cast it and compared it to various favorite graphite rods until well after dark. Coh decided that he wanted "something that nice," but left the decision up to his friend. The inherent advantage of a custom cane rod can seem overwhelming, too many choices.

We discussed tapers while driving home with twenty twelve-foot culms of bamboo on the canoe rack, and David brought out the planing form today. Then he brought out the traveling lathe and mused over the taper while turning a few experimental western juniper reel seats to the size of some Bellinger down locking hardware, and still put off the inevitable by planing the twelve waiting strips uniformly to "clean them up." The taper actually is the one thing that makes the entire rod.

Finally, he decided to go with a Payne 98 taper, to give Coh just a little faster action, and it was done. He graphed the five-inch increments for the butt diameters, then listed the half diameters, adding a safety factor of .030". To actually set the planing form, a depth dial indicator with a sixty-degree point on it is used along a slot running the length of the form. The planing form is a five foot pairing of 3/4 by 3/4 inch cold rolled steel, beveled for sixty degrees along the slot where the two are paired. One side of the form has a finer slot for tips; the other is wider, for butts. The two pieces are joined by alternating three fasteners: a hexheaded pullingcapscrew, which goes entirely through both pieces and pulls them together; a pin to keep the two sides aligned; and a recessed allen-head screw, which extends through just one strip and pushes on the other strip, forcing them apart. This allows for fine adjustment to fit the tapers. Most tapers are written down in five-inch increments, and the planing form must be set at half the diameter at each five-inch station. When six triangular strips are arranged together in a hexagon, their points are together at the core of the rod. Each triangle extends only to the middle, and is, therefore, half the diameter of the rod.

David is using the kitchen counter as his Michigan workbench, and has a four-inch wide strip of R.V. accessory material beneath the form to keep it from sliding. The form is just far enough back from the edge of the counter for a long strip of masking tape to lie like a yardstick beside it. On that strip, the desired measurement for each station is written, so quick checks with the depth dial are accurate and easy. Of course, avoidance behavior can be employed right up until plane meets cane, so tuning up planes and blades can take some time, if desired.

David has three planes, a professional grade Stanley and two Lie-Nielsens. The Stanley is made in England; his is a 6 1/4-inch twenty-one degree plane, with a 1 5/8-inch blade. He discarded the blade that came with it and substituted a Hock blade. The Lie-Nielsen planes come from Warren, Maine. We enjoy the luxury of picking them up at the foundry; their regular angle, adjustable-mouth block plane isn't in their catalog and comes ready to use. We didn't get the rodmakers' version with the center groove that avoids planing form scrapes because it seemed better to try parallel tape to protect the form, first. The other Lie-Nielsen is a scraping plane, and its makers claim that it was inspired by the Stanley #212, an ideal tool for sizing fly rod sections.

Minute slices require sharp blades. Using a fine stone, a honing guide, and an angle setting jig, David sets the primary angle at thirty-five degrees and backs off one degree for the secondary angle.

There is a trick to holding the plane level and using sufficient pressure to shave the cane strip. Tipping the plane to one side results in an uneven triangular taper, so David spot checks the diameter of each strip throughout its length after every pass of the plane. His digital caliper measures to ten thousandths. With the planing form set to be oversized by .030", and his patient re-checking and re-measuring, he's done all he can to prevent the disastrous over-planing of a strip. After a while, we realized that we'd been dead serious for a long time. David raised an eyebrow. "After all," he says, "this is the one thing that could ruin the entire rod." Kodiak came out from the living room to see why we were laughing.

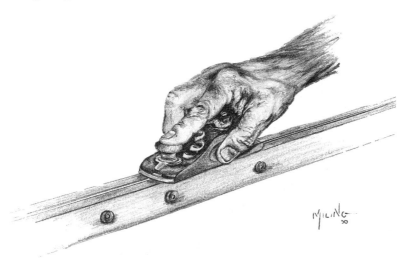

July 13, Tuesday, 9 pm

Already, David has the six butt strips planed to the
.030 tolerance and has bound them to check to shape of
the rod. He lightly sanded the enamel side with a small
block and 220 grit paper to remove the residuals of the
nodes, the debris from flaming, and the remnant curve
of the original culm, sanding with the length of the strip.
Coh will be surprised if the blank is ready for him to see
next Thursday.

This incredible weather doesn't improve those odds.
We're in the high pressure between hot and muggy
systems, with blue skies and 72 degrees. The hay is
growing back for a second cutting, but it's still short
enough for long easy walks with Kodiak. Friday night
our niece Barbie added her ten year old perspective to a
trek behind the barn while David and our friend Crewf
caught up on old times, and we tested out our new two-
way radios. It was a good thing we had one with us since
a pair of bald eagles appeared from behind the trees in
the back field, too low to be seen from the house. We
radioed the alert while the eagles rested in the swamp
trees to the north. When they gained altitude, all four of
us shared the sight.

Deer are everywhere, but are especially beautiful
grazing the new alfalfa in the low light of dusk. Twin
fawns sleep on the east side of the big bale at the foot of
the long hill behind the barn; they must have the first
rays of the morning sun to warm them. The deer have
been here all of my life, and their numbers had sky-
rocketed before I graduated from high school, but the
eagles are new and are an incredible success story since
their recovery from the days of DDT thinned egg shells.
The coyotes and wild turkeys are new, too, and seem to

be connected. Last year, we saw a coyote trailing a flock of three hens and eighteen chicken-sized young. The coyotes yap and bark together after dark to the west of the house, adding magic to the night and making Kodiak frantic. He likes the turkeys better and loves to scatter a flock on our walks.

Today, the wildlife takes a back seat to the clouds, towering, beautiful white cumulus against a blue sky. They dwarf the barn and look like mountains over the fields. The two hundred-foot tall communications tower to the north is tiny in the foreground.

David is re-setting the planing form to its final specifications and preparing to plane the butt strips to their final diameter.

July 15, Thursday, 11 pm

The planing form might not be cooperating; the butt strips just won't shrink to that final diameter as they should. David switched to the Lie-Nielsen scraper plane, and then resorted to a razorblade scraper to tweak them into submission. This is a new form, not the one he used on my rod, and may not lie square as the two halves are adjusted. The depth dial says otherwise, so the mystery persists.

The heat and humidity of the afternoon have given way to evening crickets and a gentle breeze. Redwing blackbirds, meadow sparrows, and bob-o-links are in a subtle competition. I've been seeing meadowlarks in the fields every day, but I have yet to hear their song.

Last evening, we fished the upper reaches of the Manistee River. The sand bottom seemed less troutlike than the fast, clear water, but the water tells the truth. David released two bright, chubby brookies and a small brown, and I released a small brook trout, all in the fifteen minutes between the time we stepped into the water and the arrival of the thunder and lightning. Kodiak was with us. We invite him along only if we're sure they'll be no other anglers on the river; we like to be polite. He's a good fishing dog, but he's not quite so adept at judging bank height or water depth. As we retreated, we called him out from the brush on the opposite bank. He ran right off the edge of the high bank, stepped on the surface of the water for a fraction of a second, and disappeared in the river's curve. He was a bit sheepish when he surfaced.

After three hours of tweaking, the strips were pronounced "good enough for now," which probably means close to perfect. David put them up for the night by arranging them together as they'll be as a rod butt, and binding them in place with a cotton cord twisted in a spiral from butt-butt to butt-tip and back. He rolled the bound section on a flat surface to assure that it was straight, eyed it thoroughly, and put it away for the night. It's nearly a peaceful end to the day, except for the vacuum cleaner work that follows as he cleans up the planing form and the floor. He also washes the stones he used to sharpen the plane blades and empties that water before calling it a night.

July 17, Saturday, 9 pm

David reset the form and re-marked his masking tape, then planed the tip strips to .030" over size, after only a bit of avoidance behavior. There was just a little re-sharpening and stewing about good-naturedly. After the planing, he bound the tip and hanged it next to the bound butt. The cane is at the point where the really severe avoidance behavior seems to kick in. He has to re-set the form for the tiny specifications necessary for that last .030" on the tip section and try to predict if nodes will lie under the tip top or under the ferrule. What will happen if he turns down a node on the lathe? A brief but explosive end to the entire tip? It's a good point to wait until morning and re-think it all.

July 20, Tuesday, 10 pm

David decreased the taper on the planing form for the last time and colored the edge of the scraper blade with black felt marker ink, so he could monitor his progress in sharpening it, before I woke up yesterday. It's just as well, since I'm somewhat reluctant to enter the kitchen-turned-rodshop while he's working on those ultra fine tip strips. He couldn't get the taper fine enough with the scraper plane and the form, so he used a hand scraper and then some very careful, single direction sanding to reach a satisfying diameter. By three yesterday afternoon, he was laying the numbered tip strips in order on a piece of masking tape, rolling them into a hex, and removing the masking tape. Using his foot on the string to maintain appropriate tension, he spiral-bound the tip and hanged it next to the butt to await gluing. Phew!

July 21, Wednesday, 11 pm

Anything north of the knuckles across the palm of Michigan's mitten is "Up North," and that's where we are. The Upper Peninsula is north yet of here, but this is where the bulk of the traffic is headed on Friday nights all summer long. I doubt that I've ever taken this area for granted, or ever doubted that the weekenders show good taste in coming north, but I'm glad that we have the week days to enjoy the fields, woods, creeks, and roads more like they were when we were growing up here. The hills are rolling; the forests alternate with small cornfields, hayfields, or pastures, and we see wild turkeys, deer, geese, and rabbits every day. There are wildflowers along the roadside, and everyone discusses the weather.

It rained hard this morning, so we went to town to find dowels to try in the Garrison binder. This binder spirals cotton string around the glued tip or butt strips in much the same way David did manually each time he stored them. There is a counter weight system in the binder, however, that wraps the string a lot tighter. It is driven by cranking a wheel which utilizes a cord as a belt. The tip or butt section is looped in the cord. The actual binding string is attached directly to the tip or the butt, and the cord belt rotates the section of the rod, winding the string along its length until David switches the loop, and it spirals the other way.

The problem today was to create that drive belt. It needs to be roughly an eighteen-inch loop, but the knot can't be at all obtrusive. We tried sewing braided nylon mason line, or chalk line, tensile strength seventy pounds, with an overlap of 1/2-inch, then one inch. Even with singeing the remnant ends of the nylon, which

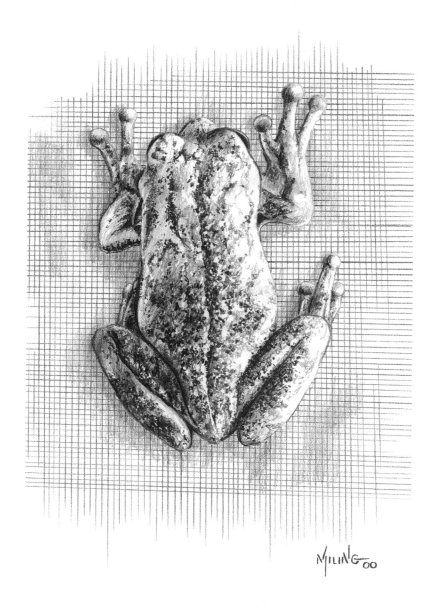

proves to be simple to melt right through, the first belt was only marginally successful on a dry run binding the practice dowels. David tied a blood knot next, which was promising if again only marginally successful. Just melting the ends together didn't hold up at all. We retired the problem for the evening with three potential belts made. It would be nice to find some hollow braided dacron, or nylon down rigger or planing board line, seventy-five to eighty pound test, or even some braided kite string, so we could work a needle up the center for a smoother transition.

There are three green tree frogs on the screen door tonight, and I can hear distant voices from the lake. Hicks Lake has always been a focal point in my life, despite the teasing its name provokes. While the part of the farm adjacent to this house doesn't quite touch it, my grandparents settled the land on the other side, now including nearly a half-mile of the last undeveloped frontage. My father and step-mother farm there now. The highlight of this summer for me may have been Monday night's fishing trip on the lake with my dad and David. Bluegills are always cooperative and fun on a fly rod, and the company was ideal. David and I began fishing with fiberglass as children, after the Cold War embargo of bamboo from China. Both of our fathers had fished with cane. Dad resurrected his old Montague, still in mint condition, and his automatic reel. The poppers he used when I was a child still provoked a big bass into exploding out of the lilypads.

July 22, Thursday, 1 am

We conceded defeat after yesterday's beltmaking. Four hours was enough. We drove to a local sporting goods giant for 135 pound, braided, hollow, planing board dacron. David threaded it through a darning needle, then inserted the needle up through the hollow core and out the side of the dacron, about 1 1/2 inches up. He pulled out the needle, leaving the other end of the dacron cord nestled inside, and then sewed through both layers of dacron with nylon thread to secure the end. He melted the fraying end as it surrounded the inserted end. This seems to make a strong belt and worked well on the practice dowel.

At 1 am, Coh and David are the last up and are in the kitchen-turned-workshop immersed in rod talk. Also our weekend guests, Janet and the girls are asleep. So is their beagle, Huck. So is Kodiak. It is exceptionally beautiful outside tonight. Fog lies low over the rolling fields, illuminated by a bright half moon, brilliant yet still allowing hundreds of stars to ring the horizon. There is a soft chorus of crickets and then the clatter of a heron. In the distance, across the lake, one of Dad's cows is lowing. Magical.

September 6, Monday, Labor Day

It's a steamy afternoon back here in Maine, and time to resume rodmaking. It seems like quite an interval since July, but the time in between did contain some research and development, better known as fishing. We packed up my bamboo rod, some graphites, and Kodiak, and headed to Wyoming.

Inclement weather kept me from trying out my rod in the high country of the Medicine Bows, but conditions were right on the upper Green River near the Wind River Range. I wish I could say that I was successful on the first cast, but I had to settle for the third. None were big, but I released a dozen trout that first day fishing cane, and I felt great. The transition from my little graphite rod to a seven-foot Payne 97 4/5 wt was easy, although I had a little trouble getting the knack of using a fine tippet. On my six-foot, 3 wt, I could always set a fly down gently with a burly leader, which usually went where I cast it. Casting a long, light leader and tippet was more challenging. It didn't help a bit when the wind blew my fly into the willows overhanging the bank; for my trouble, I retrieved it chumming the water with caddis flies. No one was looking.

The Wind River Range draws us back again and again, even after we've fished Alaska or tried other adventures. The Winds have spoiled us with their high alpine beauty and solitude; there's nothing like having our own mountain lake dimpling at sunset. A couple of summers ago, we'd tried a trail that led high and then disappeared. We literally dragged our backpacks up a steep ridge, hoping to complete the bushwhack before some thunderstorms arrived. At 12,000 feet, we found the lake and forgot the pain. The storms were holding off, and we set up the tent where we could watch for lightning, big horn sheep, and the first rises on the water. I had my spot picked out, a boulder on the shore that jutted out ten feet to where the bottom dropped off into darkness.

Then three cowboys showed up on horses. We heard them coming in time to wander over to the lake and stake claims below our tent, so they headed to the opposite shore and dismounted. I doubted if they realized it, but a little friendly competition was due. The fish might not be hungry, but I had worked harder to get to that spot, and I would fumble tying on flies all day if that's what it took to keep it. What's more, they were fishing with lures and already showing me up. They'd hoot and laugh landing their trout, and I waited for mine.

Dimples finally appeared, and David caught his first fish. He was releasing it when I saw a series of large rises, slowly headed my way. They were even and regular, and I was sure that I'd find a way to mess up the situation. I did my best to drop a size 18 parachute caddis gently, right in the line of fire. It was a big fish, especially on my 3 wt rod. I made a dozen deals to release it quickly, if only I could bring it close enough to touch.

It wasn't until David snapped the picture and the fish was gone that we noticed the storm closing in and retreated to the tent. We heard the horses approach our shelter, and I stuck my head out to see if the cowboys needed help in the downpour. That wasn't why they'd ridden over. As I looked out, they stopped, and the nearest horseman tipped his hat and said, "Nice fish, ma'am."

This summer, we found classic western fishing in a creek up on a high pass. We had avoided backpacking this area, since dogs and the local fauna don't mix. Equipped with a hard-shelled cap on our four wheel drive truck, sleeping with both Kodes and the grizzlies seemed more feasible. The climb up the dusty switchbacks was worth it. We had cutthroats and brook trout, the calls of the wolves on the ridge to the west, and plenty of nearby curiosities for Kodiak to explore. David worked a pool while I used sagebrush for cover and stalked a big trout downstream. We stayed close enough to assist each other with CPR, catch, photograph, and release, and were happy until twilight. Then we drove off to park the truck in a small stand of subalpine fir someone used when elk hunting. Crawling into the bed we had made on a shelf in the back, geared stowed underneath, the three

of us were safe and content for the night and ready for weeks more.

The second day, we lost the transmission in our new truck, throwing a curve into our trip. Twelve hours of misadventures found us at a dealership in Idaho Falls, and the second day of mechanic work landed us in a motel with a rental car and only a fraction of our gear. We had even less of our optimism, but that changed after a trip to Twin Bridges, Montana, and a long afternoon's chat with cane rodmaker Jerry Kustich. Unique pursuits can be lonely ones; there's amazing energy in finding a kindred spirit. We checked out the Madison, Henry's Fork, and some choice alpine lakes, hiked in to some abandoned gold mines, and drank from a naturally carbonated spring along the old Oregon Trail. We eventually retrieved the truck and made our way back to Maine.

Maybe there is a reason it's taken six months to glue up this rod. Like all of rodmaking, it takes some skill, and this part seems especially messy and nerve-wracking. David carried the Garrison binder and experimental belt out to the corner of the deck. Just a few leaves are changing, to belie the temperature, and the breeze makes it necessary to anchor everything tight. The portable bench top is just at working height on the high side of the deck if he stands on the ground. David covered it with waxed paper well-secured with masking tape.

The butt of the rod was unstrung, although the masking tape still held the six sections flat and in nice rows. David sanded the upright edges, which will be the core of the rod, to make a slight hollow for the glue. Using a sanding block, he can do all six sections at once. He did the same to the tip and then stashed it indoors for later.

51

Glues are a matter of much interest on the list serv, and Ron Barch had given David some resorcinol. It's supposed to have a four-hour viscous life for gluing and therefore buys some adjustment time. We mixed four parts of the molasses colored liquid, two parts of the tan powder, and one part of denatured alcohol, deeming a teaspoon a part, after some discussion. I stirred while David prepared a bucket of water for clean-up and laid the butt section, open again, enamel side down on the waxed paper.

With an old, soft toothbrush, he brushed on the glue, staining the inside of the bamboo a deep red-black. It seemed to be setting fast, so we hurried the sections back into a butt and placed the large end in the binder.

The idea with the binder is to wrap size 16/4 cotton cord, under tension, in a spiral of wraps 1/2 inch apart for the length of the butt, then switch the drive belt and wrap in the same direction again, with the cord spiraling the opposite way. The glue is squeezed out the length of the butt as the six sections are bound tightly ogether. The belt gets gluey, and so does the binder to some extent, but everything cleans up with water if there's no dawdling. As soon as the butt was wrapped, and he had rolled it on a flat surface to make it straight, David handed it to me. I carried it inside to hang up by the loose cord ends, held by half hitches at the end of the butt, and brought out the tip.

The entire process took only an hour or so and had just enough tension, just enough demand for careful technique, to make it exhilarating when we surveyed the glue covered, cord wrapped sections hanging from the clothes rack. As it turned out, the rain that had been threatening all day from the remnants of the most recent hurricane held off to materialize until after dark. Maine doesn't get many direct hits during hurricane season. By then, we had stowed all of the gear and headed out, and I had narrowly avoided hitting a moose, which also seemed to have materialized after dark.

Moose don't usually run out in front of cars; they stroll out on incredibly long legs. This one actually leaped out behind David, a misty pair of truck taillights just ahead. Kodiak and I were following in the car. I had the dims on and only saw its front legs when its hooves hit the white shoulder line. I braked, pulling to the right, with Kodiak barking orders from the rear seat, and the moose was in my lane as I went by it. I could see its rump out my side window, too close to even see its tail. Since I was already slowing on the shoulder, it seemed like a good idea to stop and take stock of life and the universe. Must be the fall rut has already begun.

Part Three

Autumn

*"Of course bamboo fly rods are heavier;
the rodmaker pours his soul into them.."*

Joe Amaral
Canadian Rodmaker
The Grand Gathering 1999

September 13, Monday, 6 pm

Along with five inches of rain on Friday came both relief from the heat and the beginning of fall. Ferns have turned brown, and the leaves on the poplars are considering a change. The mountain ash is the jewel of the clearing. The wood ducks, the jewels of the pond, fly up now in family flocks of a dozen here, a dozen there. Baby snapping turtles emerge from the soft soil under the new blueberry bushes, wipe the sand from their eyes, sniff the air for direction, and begin the long journey down to the pond. It'll be a few years before they can swim, but they'll use the sedges in the shallow water for support and for cover from predators. The horned owls began their autumn serenade of the beavers last night. The stress must be off the beavers with their pond full of water again.

After a week of curing the bound sections on the clothes rack, or occasionally outside on the clothesline,

the rod and the rodmaker were
ready for the unwrapping.
Holding each rod section in
his upright fist, a loose end
of the cord lying between
his first and middle fingers,
David tested it for straightness
as he freed the cord. In a continuous motion, he pulled the
loose end with his free hand,
spinning the section with no
apparent wobble. Straight!
"Good thing," David grins in
mock relief, "since this is the one
thing…"

It's curious how the rod
looks its absolute worst at
this point, covered with dried
glue and tracks from the
cord, but how it will look its
absolute best quite soon. For
tonight, David placed a section
in the rough planing form
and sanded it with 220 grit
paper, just enough to see a hint
of the real rod emerge. It will be
beautiful.

September 16, Thursday, 8 pm

The rain has been steady all day, and the forecast is for it to intensify throughout the night as a tropical storm passes by. When we saw the hurricane's projected path two days ago, David decided to forego our walk and work with the 400 grit sandpaper outside until most of the dried glue on the rod was gone. Kodiak and I followed the trail around the pond to the south where the Grass Dam is overflowing with fresh, clear, autumn water. The lady ferns are a gentle yellow, and the grasses have dried back on the pathway. The beavers must be working all night to pile so much fresh mud the length of the dam. I've borrowed a few of their sticks for balancing staffs, keeping a stash at both ends of the dam. There's a single bright red cluster of jack-in-the-pulpit berries near another small dam, just west of our property, and I've found pods of seeds on drying lady's slippers.

Today's rain has put an end to sanding outside, so David and I pulled on the rain gear and walked down to watch the water flood over the dams. Another inch of rain has fallen since we emptied the gauge at dusk. After our walk, David built a fire in the stove, and we pulled up the rockers to watch the flames. Coh is deciding on the hardware for his rod and will send it from Michigan, so we have time to enjoy conversations on the rodmakers' list serv and to think about the next rod, maybe a three piece, probably nodeless.

Kodiak moved close to the stove to dry off, and David joined him there to glue up Coh's grip. He used an eight inch carriage bolt with a wing nut and large washers at each end to align the corks for the grip. On it, he placed thirteen half-inch sections of cork, selected to avoid cork with holes which could become pits when sanded down. These are glued with Tite Bond II, a weather resistant wood glue, and then tightened together. The grip will be six and one half inches long.

Some evenings just can't get any better. The cork tightened on the carriage bolt has passed all initial examinations. The fire is bright and warm, and the rain outside is drumming in the quiet spaces between Bob Seger's ballads. The popcorn is almost done.

September 18, Saturday, 6pm

The beavers felled a large ash near the Grass Dam last night. Standing in the sunlight today surveying the scene, it's easy to imagine them in a panic as the cumulative results of seven inches of rain flood over their dam and them downing the big ash in a last ditch effort to salvage the situation. I suspect that the truth is a less comical scenario; the upper branches are missing, and there seems to be new sticks protruding from the food cache out by the beaver house.

Today David replaced the carriage bolt with a pen mandrel and used the lathe and some sandpaper to smooth the grip. At this point, he's settled on one inch in diameter, using 300 and 400 grit papers. There's an almost invisible line in one of the cork sections, which bothers him, but none of the cork the length of the grip has had a bad pit emerge.

The rod looks nearly ready to dip in varnish. David sanded the enamel cautiously with 400 grit paper, taking care to keep the sanding block straight and preserve the edges of the hexagonal cross section. After two hours of delicate work, he decided to rest a bit and consider whether or not it was done. While he mused it over, we took the small lathe out to the picnic table to face the small end of the butt section, left irregular until now. He wrapped masking tape on the rod's contact points with the chuck, and I steadied the long end while he held a razor saw to the cane. The newly exposed end is wondrously full of power fibers.

September 19, Sunday, 8pm

Crisp, fall-like days are invigorating. There is energy to burn, and everything is more fun, especially labors of love. We were working on the rod at the picnic table when a flock of geese flew in. We heard them coming, honking, then cruising into the pond, one splashing descent after another. The water down there is as exceptionally clear today as it is high and must seem like a smorgasbord to them. The geese are active and alert. They feel fall, too. I don't know if these are residents or southbound; we rarely see big V formations here like the continuous ones we saw daily as children in the Midwest. On our pond, we've had nesting pairs, or the same nesting pair more than one year, always out by the beaver house or in the Valley of the Dead. I wonder if these are related.

David is devoting any free time to this rod now, and his fever is contagious. Today he showed me how to glue up cork for a grip, my first. He's still deciding if he wants to use the grip where the tiny line has emerged.

While I immersed myself in cork and glue, David concentrated on the ferrule. The tabs on the ferrules, which allow it to slip on to the cane, come cut straight across. David used sandpaper in the slots between the tabs to round the edge of each one. The flatter these tabs fit on the rod, the more flush they'll be when he wraps them. He found a drill bit with a shank the same outside diameter as the ferrule's inside diameter. Inserting the drill bit into the ferrule allowed him to use it as a hard surface so he could pull sandpaper in a circular motion around the tabs, feathering them toward paper thin.

David also used the drill bit shank to measure the depth the cane would insert into the ferrule. This helped him determine the spot on the butt section to wrap with masking tape and secure in the jaws of the chuck. When he did, most of the cane extended through on the other side of the chuck, so I supported it while he worked. Inside the ferrule, the cane must be rounded to the correct diameter, followed by the transition to the hexagonal shape of the blank at the tabs. David cut little steps with the lathe at that point, then used a little file and some sandpaper to make the change smooth. This particular ferrule is made from a solid piece of stock, drilled so that the blind end of the hole where the cane is inserted has a conic shape from the drill tip. The conic shape helps to center the cane when it comes time for gluing. For us, gluing means a supply run to town and no more time today.

September 20, Monday, 6pm

It's hard to fit in a walk after school now and have any daylight left for rodmaking. Soon, we'll be indoors on the bench on weeknights. There were cirrus clouds this morning, predicting the front I see in the west tonight. There may be no walk tomorrow, or a soggy one, so we took more time tonight. Twenty-five wood ducks floated like corks, resting in the center of the pond, but two blacks flushed up when we'd barely reached the shore. They'll take more stealth to spy on. Perfect yellow birch leaves line the trail to the canoe landing at Big Rock Point. On the tote road behind our property, we saw signs of hunters here and there, scouting by ATV or 4X4. Most evenings, we hear someone, somewhere, sighting in a gun. Tonight an older couple passed us on the tote road, riding two up on an ATV. We all smiled.

It's remarkable how two reasonable adults gluing a grip can both miscount the number of cork rings, sort of a comradic mathematical synergy. We both stared at the grips lying side by side, the one with the tiny line and the one I made, newly glued. Yesterday's grip was definitely 1/2-inch longer, despite all of our careful sorting, grading of piles, and prioritized arranging. Fourteen corks instead of thirteen. Amazing. After discussing all of the more elegant options, we brought out the chop saw and cut the base cork off at the glueline. Thirteen corks.

David switched our revised grip to the mandrel and showed me how to even out the cork sections using 150 grit open drywall screen, taking care not to let the turning grip grab it and twist it up in the lathe. We used small strips of sandpaper, about two by four inches. To smooth it further, we graduated to 200, then 400 grit. No tiny line this time.

September 25, Saturday, noon

The glue of choice for securing ferrules seems to be Devcon's high strength, five-minute, fast drying epoxy. It isn't waterproof, which allows for rod repair a few generations from now. We glued the female end of the ferrule on the butt two days ago and the male portion on the tip this morning.

After sculpting and feathering the tabs on the ferrule, the calculator came out. The objective is to have a seven-foot rod when completed and to make each completed section equal in length. There's at least the seated depth of the ferrule to take into consideration. That entire length could be added to the tip, but the section lengths of the rod would be different when stored in the tube. The depth in question is seven tenths of an inch, and David wants to split it between the two sections. A tiny fraction, nine thousandths of an inch, of nickel silver caps the end of the male section of the ferrule, and the butt section will have the butt cap, which adds additional length to that piece. David settled on 42 9/32 inches and marked the ferrule end of the tip with the cutting tool of the lathe. He wrapped a thickness or two of masking tape on the cane to protect it from the jaws of the chuck. He built up more tape on the cane that extends through the headstock to make a tight fit and keep the cane from wobbling. Adjusting the rheostat for speed, he laid the razor saw in the guiding mark and cut off the excess cane.

It's sunny today, so we took the tip section, the ferrule, some epoxy, cotton thread, toothpicks, and a scrap of cardboard out on the deck. We were joined by a chorus of crows, flickers, and, occasionally, ducks, all seemingly aware that the end of the season is near. Today marks the first weekend of fall, and the first maples have changed, although it's still too early for leaf peepers to arrive in Maine.

David mixed the epoxy and used a toothpick to coat the inside of the ferrule and the turned down section of the cane tip. The feathered tabs of the ferrules will have excess glue to secure them to the transition zone on the unturned cane. It takes a lot of pressure to push the ferrule on, like pushing a piston against a trapped pocket of air. When the air escapes, there's a tiny but distinctive popping noise. At that point, I held the rod section horizontally, ferrule tight against the vertical edge of the deck, while David quickly wiped off the protruding epoxy and wrapped the thread around the ferrule tabs. After five minutes of pressure, the toothpick was rigidly entombed in the gleaming epoxy mixture on the scrap of cardboard, and the ferrule was presumed set. We'll wait an hour or more to take the thread off, to make sure the epoxy has cured.

While waiting, we noticed a little nip in the air. We'll have to think about bringing in some firewood and maybe getting some around for the winter after this one. Maybe we'll mow the clearing for the last time this weekend and clean out the bluebird boxes. The number of wood ducks on the pond has risen to fifty each evening, and the beaver trails look like shining spiderwebs of clear water among the lilypads and around the beaver houses. I can see evidence that their stored food has increased again, branch tips rising above the water's surface. The clear water near their houses reflects the trees so distinctly that I can see the leaves changing there, too. It's the last weekend of the regular fishing season.

September 26, Sunday, 8 pm

The essence of cane rodmaking lies in the free exchange and sharing of information by the individuals involved. It's in their gatherings, their shared publication, and in all of the e-mail from the rodmakers' list serv which David is reading tonight.

In the pre-dawn light this morning, we left to go maintain our section of the Appalachian Trail. We had heard rumors of blow-downs from the last tropical storm, and we had some white paint left to touch up the blazes which mark the trail. The full moon was still bright enough to light figures and cast shadows, and we saw an immense bull moose standing in a misty, moonlit oatfield. It seemed to foretell a great day.

Twelve hours, and fourteen sawed blowdowns, two river crossings, and thirty-odd friendly encounters with A.T. hikers later, we were back. Our neighbor and resident guide, Chris, had his canoe out in our pond, and was just finishing his duck blind. The season starts Friday, and he enjoys exclusive permission for a gentleman's hunt in return for property serveillance here. David showed him the progress on the rod, and Chris shared secrets about his private rainbow trout hotspots until nearly dark. While we thanked him for the offer and advice, we said we'd have to pass until next year. That season is pretty much over. As we talked, I decided that I need to think about storing my cane rod for the winter.

Kodiak is happily collapsed and still chasing mountain squirrels in his sleep. David and I are learning how to wax cane rods from masters we've never met but who feel like friends.

October 2, Saturday, 1 pm

I was making hot cider in preparation for an early morning on the deck at 36 degrees when David went to let Kodiak out and never came back. Chris was there. He'd been out on the big dam since before dawn and brought his ducks up to show us. I heard his stories in re-run while David retrieved coffee. The hooded merganser was one of only two ducks that flew over the dam at dawn and had perfect feathers for size 20 dry fly wings. The male woody was alone, down near Chris's blind in Duck Cove. Kodiak was interested but very respectful of Chris's young black lab, Shasta. She lay near the ducks professionally, a three-year-old now and fully trained. The flocks of wood ducks are suddenly gone, as usual when season opens. We speculated about photoperiods, ornithology, and the intentions of state regulators until Chris's coffee was gone.

The varnish in David's dip tank has turned a dark green this fall, which seems an odd contrast with the season. It surprised both of us. The new silk David had ordered came in today's mail, and we ran over to the post office to pick up another package left there. It was Coh's reel seat, but no guides or tiptop. With the tiptop, David would have been ready to dip the blank in the copper dip tank, especially made to hold and store one quart of varnish. David uses spar varnish.

In place of dipping the blank, he used a straw to extract a little varnish from the tank, hoping at least to test coat sample colors of the silk wrapped on a dowel. Instead, he found the sample of alarmingly deep green liquid. Advice from the sages was to use it anyway, but it's a perfect autumn day, and the picnic table could use a coat before winter anyway.

October 6, Wednesday, 7 pm

There's been a cold wind stripping the leaves from the trees and scattering them across our paths. I can almost smell last night's snow in the mountains. I haven't seen a duck in days, but occasional V's of geese include us in their landing patterns. The dogs are frisky, excited, and a little bit nervous. On our walk, they sniffed every marker, a balsam twig, a large mushroom, rocks jutting out from the old stone wall. It could be any rival for a marker post, fox, coyote, or deer. A bull moose has been scattering a few leaves of his own. Four feet of bark have been scraped off a maple near the lean-to site. The rut is still on. There is anticipation in the air; the first heavy frost will come tonight.

At least I can take some solace in the temperature falling. We've been invited to fish stripers before dawn, and I can't go. Dismantling the Edwards Dam on the Kennebec River in July was a milestone, a private dam removed against the owners' wishes through an effort led in part by Trout Unlimited. The en masse arrival of striped bass upstream this week was an unexpected delight. What hadn't happened in a hundred years was set right in the first season. I'm glad that one of us will be braving the cold to see it.

Tonight, David is working on the third potential grip for Coh's rod. The first two, his and mine, were quite adequate, but not satisfying. We spent last evening sorting 1/2-inch cork rings again and gluing them up. The reel seat Coh selected, a Bellinger deluxe of stabilized amboyna wood with nickel silver hardware, came with a half-inch ring of cork, which David promptly removed. He substituted two hand-selected rings of quarter-inch cork, carefully bored out on the lathe to fit the wood.

The grip he's making has a center hole 1/4 inch in diameter, but the hole will have to be tapered to fit the tapered blank better. David is experimenting with different drill sizes and the feel of various size holes on Coh's blank. The small end of the grip, its top, will probably be drilled with a 9/32nds bit, and the butt with 3/8ths, although he'd prefer 11/32nds. He may have to wrap masking tape on the rod to adjust for a 3/8ths-inch hole. It's time to pause to put a log on the fire and think it over.

October 16, Saturday, 7 pm

The grip is still on pause, but we aren't, and neither is the progression of fall. The leaves have peaked and were brilliant in the low light this evening. Evening comes at 4 pm now. Ring-neck ducks, three dozen this evening, have been resting on the pond, safely sheltered by the south beaver house. It snows and melts in the mountains but has stayed fall-like here. Every time the wind blows, there's a new, more colorful carpet on our paths.

We left early this morning for a rodmakers' gathering in Harpswell, a 1700's lobstering village on a long peninsula down on the coast. George Barnes's family has been there pretty much since it was settled, and so have the old white capes and stone walls, now decorated with fallen leaves. George is a wonderful old Mainer and an excellent host. The gathering was low key, friendly, and informative. We snacked on smoked mussels, pickled mussels, and three kinds of cheeses, all made by George, and enjoyed conversations with old hands, current enthusiasts, and beginners, about twenty in all. John Zimny helped with our silk thread question by revealing his favorites. He's been meticulous in his research, so his word is golden. It was also reassuring to us since David's experiments seem to give the same results. There was talk of glues, cork, tapers, and tools of the trade, fishing stories, and even more food. We moved outdoors after lunch to cast rods; why waste a beautiful fall afternoon?

The gathering went on into evening, but we came home to salvage a little time outside with Kodiak before dark. Down in our little field with the bluebird houses, he valiantly protected us from a large deer, just at dusk. Then he collapsed in front of the woodstove for the duration. The fire is still more cozy than necessary, but it's chilly enough outside to make it draw well.

David has been transforming a round winding check into a hexagon so that it will conform to the shape of the rod as the check butts up against the grip. With assistance from the tapered punch, he now turned his practice session last May into a beautiful winding check for Coh.

Using Richard Tyree's published calculations, he measured Coh's blank at the point soon to be occupied by the winding check, measuring across the diameter from flat to flat. Multiplying that number by 66.667 results in the number of 64ths needed, since winding checks are sized in 64ths. This rod needs a 20, but David tried a 19 and a 20 to be sure. Then, the round winding check is placed so that it straddles a slight opening in the jaws of the Pony vise, and the punch is tapped into it, converting the interior to a hex shape. To convert the outside diameter, the winding check with the punch still inside is placed in the jaws of the vise and tightened just enough to flatten two sides. Then the vise is loosened, the check and punch rotated together, and the vise is tightened on the next two sides, and then the next two. The 19 fit tightly on the rod but seemed to have a slight tear. The 20 was a little loose, but the diameter of the rod will increase when it's varnished.

More than working with the winding checks, David is working with the rod, getting to know it intimately. Every time he considers the next step or contemplates the last, he has it in his hands, examining it, visualizing its future, scrutinizing every facet, every edge. Sometimes, he looks at minute details under magnified light, but just as often, he sits in front of the fire, holding the rod, lost in thought.

October 17, Sunday, 5 pm

It was uncommonly warm today, nearly 70 degrees, so it seemed like a perfect afternoon to relax by the pond. The beavers have continued their overly ambitious attempts to raise the water level at the Grass Dam. The days when it was an abandoned dam covered with grass seem long passed. It's getting dark too early to spend potential walking time each evening on dam disrepair, and we're not even sure it's legal, but we are wary of flooding neighbors and the danger to the beavers in more than one respect. The soils under this dam rarely hold; once an entire section dropped out. Nearby, almost totally submerged, we found a beaver which had drowned working in the torrents. We were surprised how heavy the poor thing was when we carried it to a grave overlooking the pond. Even now, tiny whirlpools have excavated enough little breeches to keep the beavers on their toes until next weekend.

Reassured, we tried to poke our fingers in the ends of the little watery tornadoes. Between laughing and splashing, we rested and watched the growing flock of ring-neck ducks out on the main pond. They might have been laughing and splashing, too.

With the warm weather, a few peepers have voiced their presence, and crows in our tall pines seem to be calling to their counterparts across the pond. The crows' lack of ceremony is quite a contrast to the haunting rok of the ravens flying overhead. The warmth has stimulated another burst of mushrooms and lichens, some as colorful as the leaves they displace. The most notable arrival today, though, is the annual invasion of thousands of ladybugs. They are everywhere on the house, the picnic table, the mushrooms, the leaves. Good thing that they're harmless and cute.

Somehow, the ladybugs are avoiding the lathe on the picnic table where David is working by waning sunlight on Coh's grip. Chucked up on the pen mandrel, the grip was still an inch in diameter, and David wanted to turn it closer to 7/8ths. He used 400 grit sandpaper and tapered the top, resulting in a modified cigar shape patterned after the Garrison grips. We compared his progress to the grip on my rod. As we studied the grips, leaves drifted down, dislodged without so much as a breath of air. They landed noisily amidst their dried predecessors. A dark cloud front has appeared, a herald of much colder weather. At 6 pm, it's nearly dark.

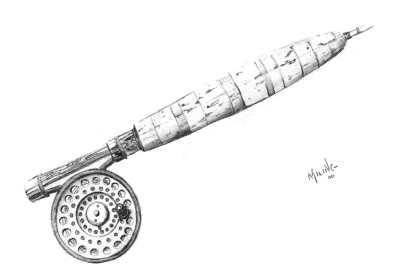

October 25, Monday, 9 pm

Fall is winding down, and there doesn't seem to be much of the year to go. The birches, a brilliant yellow, are the only colorful trees left. The beech leaves are toasted a golden brown, and the oak leaves are clinging stubbornly, a dull maroon brown. They're just waiting for the next strong wind. All of the other leaves have dried and fallen, only to be blown up and away as the breezes race up to our clearing and eddy around our firs. Great swirls of leaves rise overhead. I feel like the snowman in a snowglobe with leaves swirling instead of sparkles every time it's shaken.

We made a reconnaissance run to the coast in Saturday morning's downpour. It rained three inches in two hours, and the temperature held at 40 degrees. We were headed to a marine supply store, the largest one mid-coast, and the lobstermen and fishermen had the same idea. They looked at foul weather gear and replacement buoys; we looked at varnish.

Time-honored craftsmanship doesn't translate into old-fashioned ideas. To choose the best varnish for a cane rod, one has to understand the rod and understand varnish. There was a large selection of spar varnish and polyurethane. Urethanes are too hard; most are too inflexible for cane rods. Spar varnish will take the exterior exposures and the changes in heat and cold that sun and sleet might cause. A spar urethane is the middle ground. David used it on my rod, but he's considering spar varnish next, although he's concerned that it could melt in the trunk of a car on a hot fishing day. David flames his rods, and spar varnish tends to have a yellow color, another consideration.

We looked at Epifanes, Interlux, and Pettit, and gathered up literature on all three. We slipped into the foul weather gear section of the store and tried on sou'westers, the traditional black headgear of the inclement Gulf of Maine, complete with long back brim. The coast was certainly raw all morning and hadn't improved by noon when we stopped on the wharf for hot clam chowder before heading home.

Today a fax came from a rodmaker in England, a contact made through the list serv, detailing the specifications of Epifanes. We were discussing its pros and cons this evening when we thought we heard a muffled crash from down the hill toward the pond. I looked out in time to see Kodiak racing in that direction, forgetting he was tethered until it was too late. After a little comforting, he came in and devoured his entire bowl of food. Recreating the incident, we've since decided that the beaver splash we heard on our way indoors, just at dusk, may have signaled one heading this way. A phenomenal two hundred ring-necks were on the pond between the beaver's house and ours tonight, and they were somewhat spooky. They'd fly short distances in great flocks whenever we approached. After hearing the beaver splash, we heard the ducks all fly up and land again, sounding like a great applause when they touched the water. The beaver must have been coming over toward our house, and probably spent the next half hour felling a tree nearby. Maybe we've answered that question about the tree falling in the forest.

October 28, Thursday, 8 pm

With a little help from the small lathe, some masking tape, and some sandpaper, David started lapping the ferrule tonight. The male half, on the tip section, must be carefully sized before it will fit into the female half, affixed to the butt section. Too loose, the fit will be sloppy and ruin the rod. I inspected it carefully. "Hmmm," I asked to make him laugh, "Could this be the one thing that ruins this entire rod?"

Once again, David wrapped the point where the cane would be held in the lathe with masking tape, creating a chuck-proof barrier. Then, he carefully threaded the tip through the chuck and secured it. Using 1200 grit paper, he cautiously reduced the male ferrule by a minute fraction, removed the tip from the lathe, and tested the fit. Still too tight. He wiped the ferrule clean, tried it again, and tested it again. It's the work of great patience but has a thrilling reward. The precise moment arrives when the ferrule begins to fit, and he gets the first feel of the rod as a whole. I tried the new blank, gingerly, and was amazed to find how light and responsive it was already.

The first taste is enough for tonight since we were up in the wee hours this morning listening to the coyotes celebrate the bright moonlight. David and I were listening; Kodiak was beside himself. IIc was eventually persuaded to tolerate the moment. We all slept lightly until our usual 5:15 alarm; David and I hoping to hear more, and Kodiak worried about it.

There are well over two hundred ring-neck ducks on the pond as the daylight fades, their swelling numbers a point of real curiosity. They're harder to count now. If we show ourselves at all, they fly up and leave the pond for the night. The poplars are dropping their leaves, painting all of our paths a muted yellow.

Part Four

Winter

"The journey is the reward."
A Taoist proverb

November 1, Monday, 7 pm

We're back on Eastern Standard Time, so it's dark by 5:30. Without snow or the moon, it's very dark by seven. November is a good month for watching sunsets before supper and stargazing before bedtime. As for our walks with Kodiak, we wear headlamps, and he sticks pretty close.

Other projects progress, but the rod will move slowly this week as David waits for more of Coh's chosen components to arrive. Kodiak is watching the fire tonight as David examines the ferrules. Earlier, he coated the feathered ends of the mounted ferrules with spar urethane. Then he sanded it off so that the spaces between the feathers were even with the feathered tabs, making a smooth, uniform surface for the wraps. He used masking tape to protect the blank from the grip of the rod-winding jig and selected the thread for the lap, Pearsall's Gossamer silk in white. The silk is so fine that it lies flat and tight with very little effort. Under the magnifying light, he wrapped silk an equal distance up on to the ferrule and below the ferrule on to the rod.

David thinned the spar urethane with mineral spirits, half and half, and heated it in the microwave until he could just feel that it was warm. Then, using a dubbing needle from fly tying, he carefully coated the silk. It virtually disappeared.

November 7, Sunday, 8 pm

There are different ways to find wilderness. There is wilderness of place; for that, we sometimes travel to remote locations, either somewhere north or somewhere requiring a great investment in effort. There is also temporal wilderness, wilderness of time. Anglers know both of these. For us, off-season wilderness has elements of both. The abandoned logging roads we were exploring this morning were also abandoned today by the hunters. Maine practices a universal armistice on Sundays. These roads have been long deserted by backpacking leaf peepers, and it's too early for snowmobilers. There is another a kind of wilderness, one created by weather; most people wouldn't be out high in the mountains in the wind and snow squalls we had today. We had gone once again in search of the elusive bushwhack to the southern end of the Appalachian Trail section we maintain. Our usual access requires a precarious river crossing we find a bit chilly this time of year. We didn't discover a short cut, but we did find an isolated, gin clear mountain pond with boulder strewn rapids and deep pools in the outlet stream and 360 degree views.

It was sunny and forty degrees back here at 3 pm. Our pond is ringed with a thin layer of clear ice, extending fifteen feet out from the shore. The ring-neck ducks are everywhere. They are more skittish than before and rise in three waves, three great and beautiful ovations. Today, we counted over one hundred in each one. They circled and departed to the south. Just before sunset, at 5 pm, David walked Kodiak down to check the beavers' handiwork at the dam. A fourth ovation of ringnecks departed. Then David decided to varnish Coh's rod.

We thinned spar urethane with pure turpentine, 850 ml to 175 ml, before refilling the long copper dip tank. David put a small steel ball in the tank so he could stir the mixture when necessary and left some room in the tank for rod displacement. The tank is held in place, upright, by a fitted wooden clamp on the workbench. The rod-winding jig is on the bench. David fastened one end of a cord to a 3/8 inch dowel held in the jig. When the jig turns, the cord winds slowly around the turning dowel. The cord runs from the dowel up through a small pulley on the ceiling and back down through a pulley where a rod section will be attached and lowered into the tank. The cord continues back up to an anchor point on the ceiling.

With the cord fully wound on the dowel, the suspended rod section hangs just over the opening in the tank. Engaged, the motor lowers the rod at the rate of five inches a minute until the ferrule reaches the varnish. Then, David reverses the motor, and the rod is drawn out of the tank. We're both smiling. The rod gleams with its first coat of varnish, sparkling like the new ice under this afternoon's sun.

November 18, Thursday, 6:30 pm

One advantage of arriving home in the premature darkness every day is being greeted by a rollicking chorus of coyotes before five o'clock. They could have been at the lean-to site across the pond, or farther back, near the tote road; we didn't want to bother them or risk a canine territorial dispute. We had time to stall. No amount of rushing can get us out with Kodiak in daylight in November, anyway.

By the time we reached the Grass Dam, our eyes had adjusted to the tunnel vision of headlamps, and we regained our orientation. Darkness is its own kind of wilderness. We seemed to have reached a compromise with the beavers over the height of their dam. They've allowed the water level to lower just enough to make a dry pathway and keep clear of the neighbors, and we've stopped worrying about their handiwork. I borrowed one of their sticks to use as a hiking staff and was amazed when it ricocheted off the water. Transparent ice. Even with the headlamps, the leaves on the bottom are more defined than the ice above them.

At the lean-to site, Kodiak checked his markers with no apparent concern for coyotes. We had some concern for his safety, but it had nothing to do with rivals. Kodiak can be enticed to venture out on to the ice. Last year, we were standing at the lean-to site when we realized he was missing. We called and whistled and scrambled through the small firs and underbrush near-by, checking his favorite digging holes in snowshoe hare territory.

It was only a fluke that we looked out into Bull Moose Cove and saw him struggling. He had fallen through the ice and caught his waist on the branch of a sub-merged log, hindquarters elevated. If he dog-paddled hard, he could just get his mouth out and gasp for breath. It was pretty obvious that the closest one to him had to get out there fast; I just hoped that David could rescue me if the occasion arose. I also hoped, just for a minute, that the ice would be thick enough to support my weight. Maybe I only had half a minute to hope that; it certainly couldn't.

Adrenaline-assisted wading isn't all bad. I reached Kodiak quickly, just at waist deep, and held up his head while trying to determine the problem. As it turned out, he was so jammed I had to bend my knees to get under him and lift him out of the branch's grasp. That's when I noticed the cold. Events took a fuzzy urgency after that. Kodiak seemed very heavy, and it was harder and harder to wade. I finally noticed David saying, very clearly and deliberately, "Put the dog down." It was an inspired idea, as was offering me the end of a sapling for a tow back to shore. We three ran the half mile back to the Grass Dam and home where I discovered all sorts of black pond detritus plastered to my red legs when I stripped in front of the woodstove.

There's nothing like a good run and a warm stove to get things flowing again. Still, we don't care to repeat the experience. After tonight, we'll probably go back to the tote road for our walks until the pond freezes solid. It could be ready for ice skating by Thanksgiving, or it could melt and refreeze enough to keep us guessing.

Lying in front of the woodstove, Kodiak is either listening or expressing his irritation with the beavers. They're gnawing trails in the ice. When their channels freeze over, the beavers will continue swimming those lanes under the water. Bubbles from the oxygen trapped in their fur and exhaled carbon dioxide will keep the ice above them honeycombed. When the thaw comes, the channels will open quickly.

David is working near Kodiak. The rod has dried and hardened, so it's time to sand the varnish dull again and prepare it for another dip in the tank. There's a touch of anguish involved; the finish is beautiful. He uses 600 grit sandpaper on a block and sands in the direction of the length of the blank, using a magnifying light to constantly inspect his progress. He takes particular care with the wraps on the ferrules. He needs to dull them so the varnish can grip but wants to avoid sanding down to the actual threads, making them fuzzy. For the wraps, he uses a short, narrow strip of sandpaper looped around the base of the ferrule. Then he rotates the blank slowly under the magnifying light.

November 19, Friday, 7 pm

It was the tip's turn tonight. David used 400 grit Fre-cut sandpaper on it, which didn't seem to load up with the goo of the varnish he took off the blank. He followed that with 600 grit, pretty much the length of the blank, finding that uniform, smooth dullness needed to support the next coat. On the very tip, he used a tiny strip of the 400 grit to shape the seat for mounting the tip top. He sanded, checked the fit, sanded, and checked the fit, until the tip top seated well.

Before gluing it into place with five-minute epoxy, we inspected the blank to see if it had a spline. A spline, that slight jump a blank makes when braced on a flat surface and rolled across your hand, is well known to graphite rod builders. They debate the proper placement of the guides, on the top of the spline or on its underside, depending upon the effect desired. We were spared this debate. Coh's blank had no spline, or, in some respect, six. Not to worry, though. Guide placement then becomes an aesthetic matter, so there's plenty of room for musing, discussion, or, occasionally, debate. On this blank, we agreed quickly. David laid the blank in the wooden planing form, least attractive side up, and glued on the tip top.

November 21, Sunday, 8:30 pm

Today was oddly reminiscent of that day last April when the making of this rod began. The pond looked more like a lake again; the breezes were warm, and the sun felt good. There was even a gullible spring peeper nearby. I can hardly believe that we were scouting the mountains for ice skating potential just yesterday.

David signed and numbered the rod today. He used a .3mm rapidograph and white ink, the kind intended for acetate and photographs. His signature serves as the guarantee that the rod was crafted to his highest standards, ones that he stands behind. He labeled the rod with its length and suggested line weight for its owner's convenience and with the year preceded by this rod's place in the sequence of rods made. We both smiled as he wrote 01-99.

The tip top now firmly in place, David went ahead with the second coat of varnish. He suspended the tip from its new hardware, lowering it into the dip tank and raising it out from the opposite end as the first coat. He followed with the butt and hanged them side by side to dry, shining in the light of the woodstove. The idyllic moment and David's patience lasted about an hour. Then he had the sections down, inspecting them, and we joked about calling in sick tomorrow to work on the rod until we went to bed. With only two workdays during Thanksgiving week, we might be able to wait.

November 23, Tuesday, 10 pm

Stars appeared on the still surface of our pond as we waited at the lean-to site for moonrise tonight. At five, headlamps made tunnels in the dark. Then, a huge, orange, November moon finally rose opposite us, burning a path across the pond to our shore. By the time we walked home, I could see the colors of our jackets by moonlight.

It was another uncommonly warm evening, and we couldn't decide whether or not to go inside. Instead, we built a campfire and discussed the relative merits of bamboo rods. Everyone we know who fishes cane, fished with graphite first. We did, and we had no real complaints. But ask anglers who use both, and there are a lot of reasons they've gravitated toward cane. For us, the fact that bamboo is a living, natural material is appealing. David, a gifted craftsman, enjoys the process of cane rod creation, the precision and concentration necessary. Our library is laden with volumes he's read on the techniques and physics involved. This summer, we noticed the natural dampening of a bamboo rod; the vibration after a cast is negligible. Cane rods have more mass than graphite and don't need so much line to load them correctly, which counters the argument that graphite is lighter. Short casts are easier and more accurate, and we usually fish dry flies on small streams or mountain lakes. I'd still be a bit hesitant to climb through rough terrain or to weather mountain storms with bamboo, but I may be just a bit protective and inexperienced. Cane rods can be repaired; restoration is an art infused with the history of the particular rodmaker.

Probably one of the major reasons graphite rod builders become split cane rodmakers is the ability to control the taper. A bamboo rod can be crafted for the purpose and style of its owner by varying the taper planed into the strips. Rods can be made with fast action or slow, with a subtle hinge to assist the cast, or with variations in length for the same weight line, and vice versa. The pursuit of the most appropriate taper is attempted on paper, but casting various rods at a makers' gathering is more personally rewarding. Mention of the gatherings, of course, digressed the conversation into tangents which lingered until our campfire turned to coals.

November 26, Friday, 4 pm

The day after Thanksgiving is usually reserved for two traditions: hanging out the birdfeeders and ice skating in the mountains. This late in November, the migrant birds are usually gone. We barely filled the tube feeders with black oil sunflower seeds before the eager winter residents showed up. I like to train the chickadees to land in my hand the first day, but it rained hard all afternoon. I'm not above breaking a tradition in the face of a downpour.

Our second tradition, climbing high into the mountains in search of good ice, requires good luck with the weather, perseverance, and a willingness to risk a lot of effort only to come home skunked. It's a lot like fishing. If the weather's been cold, but not too snowy, the tarn up on Tumbledown Mountain, just west of here, will be frozen and windswept. So will the little gravel road which leads to the trailhead. Provided that we can park within a mile or two of the mountain, we can usually reach the tarn and have an hour to skate before starting back down. We take an ice axe for self-arrests and for checking the thickness of the ice, a rope for rescue (as of yet, never used), and a change of fleece clothing. Some years, we have a great climb in perfect conditions only to find thin ice or deep snow. Some years, we have a crystal skating rink at the top of the world.

This year it's sixty degrees and raining, so David dipped the rod for its fourth and final coat of varnish. Dulled from sanding, the blank disappeared into the tank and came out gleaming.

November 30, Tuesday, 9 pm

The last two evenings were successive quick steps in rodmaking, leading up to tonight. On Sunday, David removed the hood ring from the reel seat. Using a triangular file, he etched grooves in the wood where the ring resides to accept glue. He mixed some five-minute epoxy and spread some lightly on the wood before replacing the ring and setting it aside to dry. We had spent most of the day north of here, following the Kennebec River past the petroglyphs on the granite out-croppings, past the old logging booms, past the dam where the trout congregate, to the working forest.

There, Sundays after deer season mean deserted tote roads with great vistas and room for Kodiak to run. Some plantations are labeled to inform and educate the public, a less-than-subtle reminder that much of Maine's forest is privately owned, mostly by out-of-state or out-of-country corporations. There is a movement afoot to change that. Gluing on the reel seat hood fit nicely into the remaining evening.

Yesterday, David glued the reel seat itself on the end of the blank. Using 220 grit paper, he set about the grim task of roughing the glass-like surface of the last few inches of the butt. Gorilla glue is supposed to expand, foaming up as it cures. It seemed like a good way to fill the gaps between the hexagonal rod and the round interior of the reel seat. He spread a modest amount on the roughened surface, then slid on the reel seat. He laid the pairing in the wooden planing form to better align the open side of the reel seat with the intended down-side of the blank, inspecting and adjusting it until he was sure it was straight. Then, as the glue set, it foamed out the tapered bottom, filling the gaps as predicted. The excess was easy to cut off with a razor knife.

Tonight, then, it was time to glue on the cork grip. The blank looked a little naked with just the reel seat. He roughed the surface with sandpaper where the grip would be glued and used a small file to rough the exterior of the hood on the reel seat. The grip slips over the hood and slides securely against its knurl. David mixed up some rodmakers' epoxy and coated the inside of the end of the grip with the wide interior diameter where the cork would contact the hood. Then he slid the grip on the blank to a point just above its destination and coated that section of the blank with epoxy. Slowly, he moved the grip into position, wary of extruding glue. Rotating the grip until the look of the cork suited him, David made the final adjustments and then set it aside to dry. The blank is beginning to look a lot like a rod.

December 2, Thursday, 7 pm

The villages we drive through on our way home each evening have suddenly transformed. The white clapboard capes, the ornate Victorians, and the tall-steepled churches are all decorated for the holidays. Balsam wreathes have appeared on the doors; long twists of balsam garlands run down the porch-posts and columns. Peaks and gables are outlined with white icicle lights; when I was little, I'd look out from the barn through the dark, and the melting icicles lining the eves in the glow of the farmhouse windows looked just like those lights. In some New England homes, a single, beautiful candle is lit in every window. But for us, a wreath with a red bow is enough. Made from balsam tips and hung on the gable of the little porch over the front door, near the phoebe nest, it reminds us that we'll be leaving for Michigan in two weeks.

The grip and reel seat are finished on Coh's rod. Yesterday, David wrapped a little Fishhawk (YLI) silk thread around the rod to abut the grip where the winding check would go, to fill in any gaps. Then he dabbed the thread with five-minute epoxy and glued the size 20 winding check into place. It's nickel-silver and adds just a touch of sparkle to the grip. The butt cap for the reel seat is also nickel-silver. David had Coh's initials engraved on it today and glued it into place tonight. It sparkles at the other end of the grip and reel seat.

David has begun wrapping the guides on the butt section while the Kodes and I cuddle near the fire. I'm reading, and he's insisting that I scratch his ears. When the warmth gets the better of him, he drifts off and then awakens, too hot. He stands up, grinning, drunken on woodstove heat, and stumbles to the door. When I let him out, he is shocked into sobriety by the nip in the night air and prances off, woofing at the beavers. They're out in the darkness gnawing iced-in trails. If he starts barking, I scold him and bring him in by the fire, and we begin again.

David is using the Dremel tool to thin the feet of the guides Coh sent, tapering them so that the silk will make a smooth transition from the surface of the cane up on to the foot of the guide. He uses 3/0 silk, the finest size available, which lies very flat and maintains the distinct edges of blank, preserving the hexagonal look. To place each guide, he measures the butt and rolls a tiny rubber band on to the rod to mark the spot. Rubber bands, on either side of the first, roll up on to the feet to keep the guide in place.

With the rod held in the winding jig and well protected with masking tape, he begins each wrap by crossing over the end of the thread to secure it. The spool of silk is held in a bronze rod winder, based on one developed early in the century and then made popular by Herter's. It has the advantage of putting tension on the spool, not the thread, and therefore avoids damaging the silk or creating fuzzies. The silk he's chosen appears almost bronze against the bamboo.

The guide closest to the ferrule is a size 3 snake guide. The other is a size 10 stripping guide. In addition to wrapping their feet, he'll also wrap a quarter inch of silk on one side of Coh's name. That way, he highlights the rod's owner, and the thread will make a convenient measure for a thirteen-inch trout. The feet on the black guides were worn silver by the Dremel tool, so David used magic marker to color them black. It probably wasn't necessary. The silk is fine and the wraps lie tightly together.

To finish each wrap, he lays a stiff, slippery, braided loop across the threads. Over this, he winds some silk, then inserts the end through the loop and pulls the loop out, tightening the silk and securing it under the wrap. He trims off the excess silk with a fine blade. He may not finish these wraps this evening, but the rod already has the festive look of the season.

December 6, Monday, 8 pm

All six guides are on the tip wrapped with silk and varnish, drying. The tip top is a 4.5, or 4.5 sixty-fourths, measured for the inside diameter of its opening for the tip. Measuring from the tip top down, David marked the tip section at 4.5, 10, 23, 30 and 38.125 inches, and then used, respectively, three size 1/0, two size 1, and a size 2 guide. He placed the tip in the winding jig, set at a slow rotation. Then, one by one, he dabbed on the varnish using the fine point of a dubbing needle until the silk on each leg of each guide was uniformly saturated. It was the work of a long Sunday afternoon, and there will be three more coats of varnish, each drying for two days.

Attention turned back to the butt tonight. Somewhere in the confusion of the rod winding table there must be some orphan hookkeepers. They've been determined to stay lost, so David finally gave up and called Coh to replenish his supply. The makings of six strap and ring hookkeepers came today in a baggy with a long loop of string attached. On the baggy, Coh had drawn a helpful illustration, a stick figure wearing a similar baggie-necklace. Instructions read, "Hard to lose packaging, another exclusive concept."

The hookkeeper in its ultimate form will be mounted on the butt, adjacent to the grip. Before then, the strap has to be formed to allow the ring to move freely in a small, U-shaped bend in the center. The metal is very malleable and easy to shape, but the form has to be right. We looked for an appropriately sized object and tried a copper wire. David laid the tiny strap over it and used his fingers to press in the bend. Then he used smooth-jawed pliers to straighten the legs again. They'll need to be parallel to the rod's length. He slipped the ring down to the bent area in the center of the strap and held the new hookkeeper against the rod. The ring dangled too freely. The steel wire attaching Kodiak's dog tag had a slightly smaller diameter, so David tried that as the form next. It was the perfect size.

Kodiak and I were just as glad to be in by the fire this evening. We went for a walk, just before dark, but it was misty, raw, and uncomfortable outside. I was glad I had my Sou'wester. If November occasionally mimics April, early December mimics March, unpredictable and uncertain. It was 49 degrees at sunset, and the fog had settled on the pond. The ice had melted back, and the water looked black and cold. The barren trees standing out in the water made ghostly shapes in the mist. I admired their changing forms until Kodiak grew impatient with the drizzle, and the darkness sent us homeward. Once the snow comes, even a touch of starlight will light up our paths.

December 10, Friday, 6 pm

The topic du jour is the hookkeeper. David wrapped silk around the leg nearest the grip, using a blunt wooden toothpick to make sure the wraps fit snugly side-by-side. Then he pulled the other leg up and wrapped the rod under the spot where the bend in the hookkeeper will be. He slipped the ring up to the bend and smoothed the remaining leg back down on to the rod. By continuing on with the silk, the area of the entire hookkeeper was covered evenly.

The challenge comes in varnishing all of the wraps on the butt. The legs of the two guides are easy; just paint on varnish with a small brush and doctor it a little with the dubbing needle while the rod rotates in the winding jig. Wraps at 13 and 15 inches, the signature wraps highlighting also Coh's name and the statistics for the rod, are varnished the same way. The problem is to varnish the long wrap of the hookkeeper without allowing the ring to flop into the wet varnish every time the rod rotates. David tried two coats with a tiny bit of toothpick wedged between the ring and the silk. The ring didn't move, but a small area of silk under the toothpick couldn't be varnished. For tonight's third coat, he rolled a small cigar of masking tape. Inserted through the ring, it seems to prevent it from flopping over on to the drying wrap. I wondered about laying the rod in the jig with the ring dangling down and then dubbing the ring with varnish. When it dried, the ring might be frozen into place until it was broken free after the wrap was dry.

We passed on our walk tonight. It's pouring rain, and the woodstove is cheery and warm. We're watching the thermometer. Will the temperature lower before the rain stops and turn our world white? Or will the rain stop first and the ice grow thick and smooth for skating?

The winding jig is rotating slowly, not far from the woodstove. The drying wraps have become deep brown jewels on the shining rod. As each side in turn faces the fire, a flash of light races up the facet, followed by the next, and the next, and the next...

December 13, Monday, 7 pm

We worked on the canoe shed just before dark, repairing a loose rafter and inspecting the roof for snow-carrying capacity. We stay at the farm over Christmas. Shaggy cows, good food, family, and friends. Although we'll be back to celebrate the new year, the weather can change a lot in two weeks. We're pretty fickle, too. One minute we were discussing which mountaintop would be best for greeting the first sunrise of 2000, the next minute we were off on a summer canoe trip to Wabakimi, Northern Ontario's newest park. The caribou and the Canadian Shield seem like our kind of neighborhood. With any luck, we can persuade our old canoeing partners, Janet and Coh, to come with us.

For now, we're preparing for snow. We found the shovels and the scoop, and the snowblower is poised in the shed. More importantly, the snowshoes are back in their places by the back door. As soon as we return, we'll pack a float paralleling the stream flowing out of our Big Dam. It's a mile north to David's sister's that way, through hemlocks and balsams, sphagnum bogs and deeryards. Occasionally we see moose; usually we see hairy woodpeckers, ravens, and the ever-curious chickadees. Last year we found the remains of a porcupine which had been uprooted by a fisher; winter quills are the best for earrings and quill boxes.

The wraps on the rod need one more coat of varnish, but they'll have to wait until tomorrow. Tonight, David is finishing some accessories. Weeks ago, he trimmed a few inches of excess cane off the butt of the rod. Last week, he chucked it in the lathe and sliced off a few thin hexagons with the razor saw. Each flat, tiny hex showed off its six component sections and their power fibers in a beautiful geometric display. He drilled a hole near the edge of one side in each hex and slipped in a gold earring wire. Tonight, he's applying the fourth and final coat of varnish to a pair which will soon belong to Janet.

Another section of the excess cane will become the ferrule plug for Coh's rod. David is planning to sand down a small piece of dowel until it fits snugly in the ferrule. Then he'll set the dowel into a hollow drilled just into the piece of bamboo. The finished plug will be about an inch long. Coated with varnish, it won't just protect the ferrule. It will be a beautiful, integrated part of a well-maintained rod.

December 15, Wednesday, 5 pm

David had the rod in his hands when I came downstairs at 5:30 this morning. He was standing in the light of the magnifying lamp, inspecting it from tip to butt. Then the smile started. It was done. We were both nearly giddy.

Normally, a rod is cast before the final pronouncement, but this rod is an exception. Rodmakers often tape on the guides so that they can test the action of the chosen taper early in the process. We would both like to cast this rod, but not the first cast. Coh had to miss so much of the rodmaking that the first cast will go to him.

We leave for Michigan in four days, exactly eight months from the April day when the serious rodmaking began. It looks like the weather should hold for the two-day drive, and we've packed the ice skates and holiday packages. Kodiak's things are ready; we'll pack our own at the last minute. Tonight we'll celebrate the journey of the last eight months. Coh's rod will be making its final trip with us. It came to Maine last January as strips of a culm of bamboo. It's going back on Saturday as a heartfelt gift for a good friend.

January 19, Wednesday, 9 pm

The snow has finally come, and the thermometer has been hovering around zero. This might be my favorite time of year. There's about a foot of snow on the pond, where the wind hasn't scoured the surface completely clear, and a foot or more of ice beneath it. Suddenly, we can go anywhere. Although the days are getting longer, it's the snowpack's reflection which illuminates our clearing when we come home each evening.

Tonight, the moon is almost full. While Kodiak waited impatiently, we pulled headlamps on over layers of clothes to prepare for our walk. We never remembered to turn them on. Snow sparkled in the moonlight in every direction as we crossed the length of the ice. Wind-shaped snow formations looked like frozen waves; the skeletons of beaver-drowned trees cast distinct, surreal shadows. Even on shore under the firs, the tracks and bunny trails in Kodiak's secret repertoire were clearly visible to us. The moonlit sights and the exercise warmed us so much that we had our mittens off before we returned.

The rod is Coh's now. We drove directly to Janet and Coh's over Christmas and brought out the rod after an appropriate amount of time greeting the kids and stalling to aggravate Coh. There wasn't a lot said, but there was a lot of grinning and gingerly passing the rod around, and some pretty long, meaningful looks that made my heart happy. We couldn't cast the rod in the darkness and wind that evening, and it poured rain the next morning. We lingered at the shop as long as we dared, then headed north. When we checked our answering machine later that night, Coh's voice said not to worry about the rod, the damn thing casts itself.

After the holiday celebrations settled down, a few days later, Coh and Janet brought their girls and beagle Huck up north. We had had snow when the south had rain, and the wind was bitter, so the adults settled in front of the fireplace downstairs while the girls joined our niece Barbie to play dress-up in the bedrooms. David's mom drove out from town and joined us, along with Barb and Duncan who had caravaned with us from Maine. Duncan and Kodiak stayed upstairs with the girls so feisty little Huck wouldn't chew them up. My dad and stepmom dropped over, then our sister-in-law and another niece. As the afternoon progressed, the cozy crowd grew, and our often-empty Michigan home was filled with good company and good cheer.

Aside from the others, Coh mentioned to David that he'd cast the rod every day and that a friend had come over to cast it, too. Bamboo in hand, his friend said that it was amazing; jeez, after all these years, he could finally cast a fly. Coh had brought the rod along, and everyone inspected it. It was too windy for us to give it a decent try and too cold out in the barns. David did tell Coh that he wouldn't worry too much about using the rod hard or taking it out in inclement weather. "Car doors," he told him, "you've got to watch out for them." He looked at me with exaggerated seriousness and big, wide-open eyes. "Car doors," he lectured, "are the one thing that can ruin the entire rod." "But," he told Coh, "don't worry about it. I'll just make you another one."

David started splitting cane again back here in Maine on New Year's Day. He's making a rod to donate to Trout Unlimited for their April auction. He may never keep one of his own rods, but with his cradle to grave philosophy, he'll never completely give one up either. Some of the techniques look easier to me this time. The list serv has offered suggestions for sources of endless pulley belts for binders and for zeroing in depth gauges that have tips made blunt by serious use. Both plagued us a bit this summer.

Kodiak is still out in the moonlight. When we reached the door after our walk, he balked several feet away. He tried to entice us back with play bows and dogtalk, but David had to go inside, and I wouldn't play. He pretended to come to my calls and then zoomed past me as fast as he could. I'd swear he was laughing. He disappeared around the canoe shed, so I crouched by the door, just out of sight. I was warm still, but my hair was totally frosted where it extends below my hood. I hope I'm still out on moonlit nights when my hair finally turns that white. Kodiak crept up from behind and then zoomed past me again. His muzzle looked white, too. I knew exactly what he meant; I didn't really want to go in yet either. Life is too short. One of us has to work tomorrow, so I wished him a fine romp and came inside.

DEMCO 38-296